Creation House is a ministry of Christian Life Missions. Its purpose is to publish and distribute Bibles, books and other Christian literature presenting the gospel of Jesus Christ. If you would like additional information, we encourage you to write to us at 396 E. St. Charles Rd., in Wheaton, IL 60188.

Living
With
Jesus
Today

Living With Jesus Today

Juan Carlos Ortiz

Creation House
Altamonte Springs, Florida

Other books by Juan Carlos Ortiz

Disciple. The first in the famous Juan Carlos Ortiz series—a book that establishes the author as a man with a message from God. Now in its fifteenth printing and published in ten languages.

Cry of the Human Heart. Second in the series and an additional development in the perceptive unfolding in the life of man and the will of the Holy Spirit. Five printings, six languages.

This book is dedicated to my wife Martha, without whose love and encouragement it could not have appeared.

Also, I gratefully acknowledge the help of David Ord in the preparation of the manuscript.

Library of Congress Catalog Card Number: 82-072240
International Standard Book Number: 0-88419-187-7

Creation House
Strang Communications Company
190 N. Westmonte Drive
Altamonte Springs, FL 32714
(407) 869-5005

Biblical quotations are used with permission from the New American Standard Bible © 1971 by the Lockman Foundation.

First Printing, July 1982
Second Printing, October 1983
Third Printing, November 1984
Fourth Printing, July 1986
Fifth Printing, February 1988
Sixth Printing, June 1989

Contents

"We have to know
beyond the shadow
of a doubt
that we have within us
all the resources
of the One
who upholds
the universe."

Juan Carlos Ortiz

1

The Eternal Babyhood of the Believer

We have a phenomenon in the church today which I call the "eternal babyhood of the believer."

We have members of our churches who, after years of hearing messages, are just the same. They continually need a minister to keep after them—changing their diapers, putting talcum on them, and checking that their milk isn't too hot. The church seems more like a hospital than an army.

Sometimes we fool ourselves because we grow numerically. We think that this is growth. But to grow in numbers is not spiritual growth. Cemeteries also grow numerically. To have a hundred people without love, then two hundred without love, is just to get fat.

Often we see the situation, but we don't know what to do about it.

We tell our people, "You should be bearing fruit for Jesus. You should be experiencing the virtues of God. You should have more love, more peace." But we cannot expect such qualities in babies. They are found only in adults.

This was Paul's complaint when he observed the lack of spiritual growth in the Corinthian church. "You are still babies," he told them.

To the Galatians he wrote that he needed to go through the pains of childbirth all over again for them.

And when the people in the book of Hebrews ought to have

been teachers, they needed to be taught the first principles over again: they could take only milk instead of solid food.

I have a little girl called Georgina. If I tell her, "Georgina, give me grandchildren," even if I pray for her, fast for her, and spank her, she cannot give me grandchildren. Not because she is naughty, not because she is rebellious, but simply because she is a child.

Of course, if she grows, she can give me grandchildren, without praying and without fasting. Because that's the natural fruit of growth.

When I was eight or nine years old, our church had a visit from a preacher who had a nice beard. Beards were not as popular in those days as they are today, so it was very unusual. I fell in love with that beard. He looked like a prince!

So I began to pray for the Lord to give me a beard. And I remember that once I had a day of fasting and prayer.

My mother asked, "Johnny, are you not eating today?" I answered, "No, Mom, I'm fasting."

"But why are you fasting?"

"It's a secret petition," I explained.

The beard didn't come, even though I prayed and fasted. But when I was 16, without praying, without fasting and without confessing, the beard came as a result of natural growth and development.

The church is no different. Growth results from life. When we are spiritually alive, we grow in love, in joy, in peace, in longsuffering, in gentleness, and in all the virtues of Christ. These are the natural fruit of spiritual life, and no amount of effort on our part can produce them.

One of the main reasons for the lack of growth in the church is the fact that we are centered in concepts instead of in life. We are very conscious of which doctrines we subscribe to, which theological system we belong to, which principles we hold to.

What do I mean by being concept-centered?

Suppose you ask me, "Brother Ortiz, will you give us a Bible study on joy?" Of course, I am glad to do so.

I go to my office, take a concordance and look for the word "joy." I put down all the verses on joy. Oh, how many! Then I take out those that will suit my message and leave the rest.

Next I look in the Greek dictionary. What is joy in Greek? Wonderful! Now the Hebrew. Oh, still better! I also see what Spurgeon, the great English Baptist preacher of the 1800s, said about joy. Nice! And I check Whitfield, and Shakespeare.

So I have my study ready. Next meeting I come and I say, "Brethren, we are going to speak about joy today.

"Joy in the Greek has a different meaning than in English, because Greek is a richer language. But the Hebrew conveys even more meaning than the Greek.

"Abraham said about joy...Jesus said about joy...Paul said about joy...Spurgeon said about joy...."

And the people say, "What a study on joy! Thank you, Pastor."

Someone then suggests, "This is such a tremendous message on joy, Brother Ortiz. Can you give us the notes?"

"Yes, we can make photocopies and give them to you."

So they fold up the notes and put them in the back of their Bibles and forget them.

But nobody has the joy! They have the concept of joy, but not the life of joy.

What do you have? The concept? Or Him who is the life?

The denomination to which I belong decided to get together with another denomination. All went well until we became a little larger and began to write our constitution.

We met in a committee. When the article on "holiness" came up, we said that we believe in holiness. But the other denomination said, "No, we want to put there that we believe in "instantaneous holiness."

"What's that?" we asked.

"Well, that you are sanctified instantaneously."

"No, Sir!" we replied. "We believe in progressive holiness."

I didn't understand the issue because I hadn't studied it before. So I said, "Listen, why don't we put both in the article: 'We believe in instantaneous and progressive holiness.' "

"No, no, no!" was the response.

So there was a division. As a result, neither of the two groups was holy in the way it acted.

In practice, both types of believers are the same. It isn't that some are more holy or less holy. There's no difference at all. It's just the concept. We didn't have the life of it, but we had to be right on the doctrine!

Some people must imagine that when we get to the gates of heaven, St. Peter is going to hand us a piece of paper with a pencil.

"Ten questions. If you get seven out of ten correct you get into heaven right away. If you get less than seven but more than four, to purgatory. Less than four, to hell directly.

"First question. Which baptism do you believe in? Immersion, ablution, aspersion; in the name of the Trinity, in the name of Jesus alone; three immersions, or to pass under a banner? Put a cross beside the right one."

What a problem! You cannot copy from those around you, because on one side you have a member of the Salvation Army, on the other an Anglican, and you are a Baptist. So the three of you are going to have different answers!

Some people make an issue of things like this, and that brings division to the church. But it's not the right way of baptism that counts. It's Jesus in your heart.

In the kingdom of heaven, they don't take doctrinal tests. St. Peter isn't going to be there with a blackboard, pencils and paper. He has a stethoscope.

Perhaps you come with all your books on doctrine to take your test. "St. Peter, where is the desk to take the test?"

St. Peter gets out his stethoscope. "Tick, tick, tick, tick."

"Get in."

"But what about the test?"
"That's all right. You have life, so you belong."

Salvation is coming from death into life. "But this we know that we have passed from death into life, that we love." Love is the manifestation of life. But usually when someone doesn't believe as I believe, there's hatred instead of love.

I'm not against theology. What I am stressing is that if you have no life, you can have the best theology, but you are lost.

Doctrines can have their place, but not the first place. That is reserved for Jesus alone. "Who has the Son, has life." Not, "Who has the right doctrines has life." But who has the right Person.

When we have Him in our hearts, and when we walk in rec ognition of that fact, we start to grow spiritually. We become more like Him. His life within increasingly shows in the way we live. As Paul says, we are being changed from glory to glory into the same image, by the Spirit of the Lord.

If you have a joy which you can lose when problems come, it has to grow until the joy overflows and nothing can take your joy away. You grow spiritually, in love, in joy, in peace, in longsuffering.

If you can love today more than you did yesterday, it means that you grew. Not that today you know more doctrine than yesterday: that is just to fatten your intellect.

Years ago when I heard someone speaking against me, I started to speak against him.

The next year, when someone spoke against me I gritted my teeth and didn't speak against him. That was better.

The day arrived when someone was speaking against me and I started to praise the Lord. That was growth.

No, we don't have to pray and fast and work and confess to be like Jesus. Growth comes naturally when we center our life in Him, and we know that He lives within us. It is His life within producing the fruit.

The ancient people of Israel were not like other nations because they were the people of God. They were a kingdom of priests which God led by the Spirit through prophets. But they wanted to be like other peoples who had kings to fight their battles.

It's sad, but the church has fallen into the temptation of becoming like any other religion.

What is a religion?

A religion has a founder—Mohammed, Buddha, Confucius, Zoroaster. The founder says things which are written in a book. When the founder dies, he leaves the book, and his followers take it and try to do what it says.

The Mohammedans have the Koran. They take their doctrines from the book. They are poor compared with us! They have only four schools of interpretation.

In our Christian religion we have a founder, Jesus Christ, who died a long time ago. The things He taught were written in the Bible. Now we take all our doctrines from the Bible as if He were dead like Mohammed.

So we have the Calvinists and the Arminians. We have the premillennialists, the post-millennialists, and the amillennialists. So many different doctrines, all within the same church. And we fight and throw verses at one another, "Take this, take that."

We act as if our founder were dead like those of other religions. In this way we lower Christ to the same level. We complain that the Mohammedans put Jesus on the same level as Mohammed; but we do just the same, because Christ is for us what Mohammed is for them.

So we make Jesus to have no word for today. He cannot do anything today. He is gone. We have His book, and that's all. But praise the Lord for the book. Because that book, the Bible, tells us He is alive!

The big difference between us and other religions is that our founder is living and is actually the head of the church. The trouble is, we don't let Him do too much. Even though we have the concept that He is the head of the church, in reality He cannot rule because everything is settled by our committees.

The church doesn't know what to do when there is a move of the Spirit. "What's this?" we say. "We must be careful."

There is panic, and problems. Divisions come. Why? Because too often the church's structures are not suitable for a living Christ. They are made for a funeral home, for a dead founder.

Often when you go to a church they are talking about the Samaritan woman, and Zaccheus, and the ten lepers, and the cursing of the fig tree, and the calming of the Sea of Galilee, and blind Bartimaeus, and the multiplication of the loaves and fishes; and the Samaritan woman again, and Zaccheus, and the ten lepers, and the cursing of the fig tree; and the Samaritan woman, and Zaccheus, and the ten lepers; and the Samaritan woman, and Zaccheus...as if Jesus had done nothing since He died.

He really must be bored to hear our sermons. They sound like funerals, because at a funeral we speak about what the deceased person did when he was alive.

A university student who was saved in our church told me, "Brother Ortiz, the first six months I was learning continually in the church. After six months I found out that I had got to the point that I knew everything that everyone else knew. I knew how the second coming of Jesus was going to be, all about the Great Tribulation, the new birth, the Trinity. From then on I was just maintained."

Lots of people don't go to church because they become bored. Not because the services are bad, but because they're always the same. The same hymns, the same messages, the same liturgy.

You really have to be longsuffering to go to all those meetings. Even God has to be longsuffering!

Many people are centered in the church's activities and not

in Jesus Christ. We go to a meeting, and we come from that meeting to a Bible study, and then to a prayer meeting. We are forever in meetings.

We even measure our spirituality by our attendance at meetings. A person who attends all the meetings is very spiritual. "Oh, he's a fine Christian. He goes to all the meetings."

But if he doesn't go to two or three Sunday meetings, "He's backsliding."

I'm not against meetings. But I do wonder what would happen to us today if all the churches were to be closed. What would happen to our religion? Christ, not meetings, must be the center of our Christian life.

Is it any wonder we don't see more growth in God's people when we are so centered in concepts instead of in the living Christ?

But thank God, all around the world there are people today who are not satisfied as they are. They are tired of trying to live like Jesus and constantly feeling like failures. They see their lack of love, their lack of joy, and they long for a revelation in the knowledge of Him, that they might be the living letters they were meant to be.

We need a new generation of Christians who know that the church is centered around a Person who lives within them.

Jesus didn't leave us with just a book and tell us, *"I leave the Bible. Try to find out all you can from it by making concordances and commentaries. Bye, bye."*

No, He didn't say that.

"Lo, I am with you always," He promised. "Where two or three gather together in My name, I am in the midst of them." He didn't leave us as orphans. He Himself is within us. "I will not leave you comfortless, I will come to you. I'm not leaving you with a book alone. I am there, in your hearts."

Paul prayed that God's people might know that Christ lives in their hearts by faith, that they might be strengthened in the inner man by the Holy Spirit.

We today need to know that Christ lives within us. We need to know that we no longer live on our own anymore but that Christ is now our life. We need to recognize that because our old self was crucified with Him, He now lives within us.

Because He is our life, we have His character in us. We don't have to try to copy, in our own effort, what the book says about the way He lived. We don't have to fast and pray that He will give us more love, more joy, more peace. We just have to know that we have the Author of the book within us, and He is all of these things.

When we know this, growth comes naturally. Change comes in our lives because more of Christ is seen. Only this revelation of Christ in us can bring about growth in spiritual fruits.

"Turn your eyes upon Jesus," we sing. In this book we are going to turn our eyes upon Jesus—as our Savior, and as our life, both individually and corporately as His church.

He is to be the center of the church, its very life!

"Lord Jesus, we turn our eyes upon You, that we might know that we have Your life within us, and that we may live that life by faith."

2

Veil of the Bearded and Sandaled One

As I read the letters of the New Testament I see a tremendous difference between the Christ whom Paul presented to the world and the Christ the church presents today.

Paul said, "Therefore from now on we recognize no man according to the flesh; even though we have known Christ according to the flesh, yet now we know Him thus no longer" (II Corinthians 5:16).

When he preached the Gospel, he didn't present the Christ of the four Gospels.

You never find him talking about the Samaritan woman, the feeding of the 5,000, or the raising of Jairus' daughter. Instead, he proclaimed the ascended Christ who is alive today, to whom every knee will ultimately bow and every tongue confess that He is Lord, to the glory of God the Father.

Often when the church preaches the Gospel, it presents the Christ of the Gospels—the Christ with a beard and sandals, who walked on the waters of the sea of Galilee, who cursed the fig tree and who healed the ten lepers.

But the emphasis in the primitive church was entirely different.

Listen to what the author of Hebrews wrote: "Therefore, brethren, since we have confidence to enter the holy place by the blood of Jesus, by the new and living way which He inaugurated for us through the curtain, that is, through His flesh, and since we have a great priest over the house of God, let us draw near with a true heart in full assurance of faith, with our hearts sprinkled clean from an evil conscience and our bodies washed with pure water" (Hebrews 10:19-22).

The life that Jesus lived on earth was to open up a whole new relationship with God for us. It was so that we could know Him as He is now, in a living relationship that is ever fresh. His earthly life was just the gateway to the new way in which we now can experience Him.

So I have asked myself many times, "Why does the church usually present the Christ of the Gospels, instead of the Christ of today?"

The Christ whom Paul preached said at the time of His departure, "Lo, I am with you always, even until the end of the age."

That Christ is eternal, and He is still with us today! He lived before He came to earth, and He is living right now, long after His ascension to heaven.

Why then do we who live in the 1980s insist on presenting to the world the historical Jesus of almost 2,000 years ago? Why is it that almost every time we preach, it is about this Jesus of the past?

The picture of Jesus in the flesh is actually the poorest picture of our Lord. The Bible says of those 33 years when He was on earth that Christ was made of "no reputation."

Paul said of Jesus' earthly life that though He was inherently God, He did not count equality with God something to be grasped but "emptied Himself, taking the form of a servant, being born in the likeness of men" (Philippians 2:5-11). He made Himself of no reputation for 33 years. The Spanish Bible says, "Made Himself nothing."

In what role did people know Him on earth?

Today He has a "name which is above every name, that at the name of Jesus every knee should bow." But on earth He was known simply as a carpenter. The eternal, glorious Christ was made like one of us, like a servant, like nothing.

The Christ who was made of no reputation "humbled Himself and became obedient unto death, even death on a cross." He not only humbled Himself to live among men, He was born in a manger like an animal. He spent His life going among sinners—publicans and prostitutes. Then He was crucified as the worst kind of criminal, and even buried in a borrowed tomb!

Jesus on earth was the bearded One in sandals and robes—a man of no reputation. So it is little wonder we are very impressed by some of the things which He did, which to us seem very great.

We are very impressed by Jesus' power when He cursed the fig tree and it died. But really, what is it for the One who created the entire Garden of Eden to curse a fig tree? It is no great feat.

You can imagine the angels up there in heaven teasing Him about cursing the fig tree. "Come on, was cursing the fig tree all You could think of doing?" To them, it was nothing. But of course, it is a great thing for us.

He also stilled the waters of the Sea of Galilee. The Jewish people call it a "sea" because it is the only body of sweet water in the country. Actually, it is just a small lake. But what is it for the creator of the galaxies to still the waters of a lake? If you have a glass of water in your hand and you create a storm in the glass, you can still it in a minute—in a few seconds, even. Well, it was no great thing for Christ to do that with the Sea of Galilee. But we are terribly impressed!

Why are we so impressed?

Because we know Jesus after the flesh. We see Him from the vantage of fleshly human beings, not from the vantage of spirit. For those 33 years He gave up His glory and became like one of us—a baby, a carpenter, a preacher. Yet what are 33 years compared with eternity? You might as well ask, what are 33 cents to a billionaire?

But it seems that the only thing we know of Christ is those

33 years. All of our Sunday School material is based on those years. I was practically born in the church. My mother committed her life to Christ before I was born. So as far back as I can remember, I went to Sunday School. I was there every week, and I heard the same material many times over.

Every five years the curriculum was completed and again I would hear the same teachings. I knew every lesson that was going to be given, and they were all about Jesus' 33 years of humiliation.

It's the same with the church calendar.

We start with Christmas. Then comes the story of the 12-year-old boy. Then there is His baptism, the temptation, the parables and miracles, and lastly the crucifixion, resurrection and ascension. Then we go back to Christmas, the 12-year-old boy, the baptism, the temptation, the miracles, the crucifixion, the resurrection, the ascension...and back to Christmas again.

Then I went to the seminary.

There, they had a subject called the life of Christ. Do you know where it started? In the manger. And do you know where it finished? At the ascension. And they called it the life of Christ! It may be 33 years of the life of Christ, but it is not the life of Christ.

Why did Paul tell the Corinthians that he wasn't too concerned with knowing the historical Jesus? It was because there was a problem in the Corinthian church.

Paul was the first one to go to the city of Corinth with the message of salvation. After he left, Apollos visited there. Now Apollos was a tremendous preacher. Many of the people gravitated to him above Paul because he was so eloquent. But after him Peter went there, and he too had a nice ministry.

Later, one group in the church said, "We prefer Paul." Before long there was a division, because the fans of Apollos and the fans of Peter disagreed with the fans of Paul. This was all in the same church! In the same body there were fans of three different men.

That kind of division occurs among babies, Paul told them. Perhaps he would have said that many of us today haven't even been born, because we can't even go to the same service! At least they were all in the same church.

"I am of Paul, I am of Apollos, I am of Peter." Perhaps the senior people in the church were fans of Paul, because when Paul arrived in the city there were no believers there at all. He had to work making tents to sustain himself. So they remembered Paul.

The young people, on the other hand, were probably the fans of Apollos because he had an intellectual capacity and charismatic speaking ability that could convince anybody. When Apollos preached, people wept.

Peter was different again. Perhaps he appealed more to the women. Not because he was good-looking, but because of his special ministry. He was an old man by this time, but he was one of the three closest apostles to the Lord Jesus when He was on earth. The Lord Jesus with a beard and sandals.

So when Peter was coming to Corinth they announced in the church, "One of the twelve is coming... one who walked and talked with Jesus. One who traveled with Him." Needless to say, the place was packed when Peter came.

Peter didn't need to prepare any of his sermons. He just told stories about Jesus. The New Testament hadn't been written yet—the life of Jesus that we read of in the Gospels wasn't yet on paper. So Peter could give people firsthand facts that nobody knew anything about.

"Dear brothers and sisters, as you know I am one of the twelve," Peter said. "I was actually one of the three closest ones. Now, every time the three closest apostles are named, we are named in the same order—Peter, James and John... Not without reason, I say this—just to show you how close I was to Jesus.

"We were walking down the street one day. We had been preaching and healing the sick the whole day, and we were re-

turning to the city in the evening. The Lord said to me, 'Peter, I am hungry.' You can imagine how I felt! I looked around to see if anybody had any food, but nobody had anything left. We had eaten everything we had brought with us. But looking around I saw a fig tree ahead of us, and I knew He loved figs.

" 'Oh,' I said, 'a fig tree.' But when we got to the tree, there wasn't one fig on it for the Master. Do you know what He did?

"No, He didn't put figs on the tree. He cursed the fig tree and the fig tree dried up in front of these two eyes!

"What power!

"Another day we were crossing the Sea of Galilee, and I said to Jesus (you know, we were very close), 'Jesus, we know how to cross the sea. We are fishermen. You sleep, because You have worked very hard.' I was very concerned for Him. So He listened to me and took my advice.

"Jesus was asleep and we were out in the middle of the sea when a storm came up. The wind blew so hard and the waves raged against our ship, and we thought we were all going to die. So I went to shake Jesus awake. 'Lord, wake up,' I said frantically. 'We are sinking.'

"So He stood up, and leaning on my shoulder—I can still feel the touch—He spoke to the winds and to the waters. And in a second the sea was calm and still."

Oh, how that touched people. They started to weep. What a miracle, what power!

Somewhere in the church somebody said to the brother sitting next to him, "Listen, why didn't Paul tell us these things? He never said anything about this."

"Be quiet, I want to listen," this brother said. "It was because Paul was not with Jesus. He was converted much later and never saw the Lord."

Peter continued. "Then there was the time when He healed Bartimaeus, the blind man...."

"Look," this brother persisted, "to be an apostle,

shouldn't a person have seen Jesus?"
"Yes."
"But you said that Paul was not with Jesus."
"Shut up and listen."
Meantime, Peter continues: "Now the Samaritan woman...."
"I don't believe that Paul is an apostle, because if he is an apostle he should have been with Jesus. This is an apostle—listen to what he is telling us!"
By now Peter was talking about the ten lepers. And the gossip had started in the church. Perhaps Paul was not an apostle since he had not been with Jesus, and one of the requirements of an apostle was to have known Jesus in person. But Peter, ah—he was an apostle!

The gossip began to filter back to Paul. What reached his ears concerned him, because like you and me he was subject to moments of anxiety. So he took a pen and wrote a letter to the Corinthians.

"From here on I know no man after the flesh," Paul said to them. He meant, "It doesn't matter that you are a doctor or an apostle. The thing that counts is your relationship with Christ, not your title."

If Paul had Peter in mind when he spoke of those who knew Christ according to the flesh, he didn't mean that Peter did not have a relationship with Christ. No, he loved Peter and respected him. Admittedly he once rebuked him in front of everybody. But he wasn't trying to put Peter down when he spoke of not being concerned about Christ in the flesh.

What Paul was getting at is that it wouldn't have mattered even if he had known Christ after the flesh—if he had been there along with Peter, James and John. "I would prefer to know Him as I now know Him," he was saying.

Do you know how Paul knew Jesus?
The first time Saul, as his name was then, saw Jesus, he al-

most died. His first encounter with Him was on the way to Damascus. The Lord opened up a window in heaven. But He was a little careless. He let too much of His glory come through, and it almost killed Paul. Paul fell from his horse and was blind for the next three days.

Later, Paul was taken up to the third heaven, to the central headquarters of the kingdom of God.

At that time he had an interview with Christ. We don't know how long this encounter took; there may have been several of them over a period of months or even years. This took place after he fled from Damascus. We don't read anything about him for many years, until the time Barnabas went to look for him in the town in which he had been born and brought him down to Antioch. But we know that he was two or three years in the wilderness, praying.

When Paul was caught up into heaven he spoke with Christ.

But not with the bearded Jesus with sandals. This was the glorious, eternal Christ. Paul saw Him in His eternal state. And this was better than to have known Him in the flesh, in the time of His humiliation, like Peter knew Him.

Peter had difficulty with some of the things Paul wrote.

"Be careful when you read the letters of Paul," he wrote one time, "because they have some very difficult concepts in them." Peter had seen Christ only from the standpoint of His earthly ministry, but Paul had seen Him in glory. So perhaps Paul had a much deeper understanding of the eternal Christ.

Like Paul, I am glad that I got to know Christ as He is now and not as He was on earth. You see, I have one problem less than those who knew Him as a human being. Too great a consciousness of the Christ in the flesh can be a hindrance to knowing Him in the spirit.

Every time those who knew Christ in the flesh prayed, they remembered what He looked like. But Paul didn't have that problem. He knew Christ exactly as He is. And this was to his advantage because for him Christ was more of a living reality than a historical personage.

It is evident when we read the letters of Paul that he never quotes the Gospels once.

For example, he never says, *"Dear Timothy, I am going to explain to you the passage about the Samaritan woman."* Do you ever read of Paul doing that? Yet we do it all the time.

When we preach the Gospel, how do we do it?

We first preach about the Samaritan woman, the ten lepers, or Zacchaeus. Then we spiritualize those stories and lead into the Gospel.

But Paul didn't do that. He encountered the apostles in Jerusalem for only 15 days following his conversion, so he really didn't know too much about the historical Jesus. He never had the opportunity to sit down and say to someone, "Explain the story of Zacchaeus to me."

If you have knowledge of the historical Jesus alone, it is retrospective knowledge—it is static knowledge.

I remember once I preached a sermon on the Good Samaritan. It was during an evangelistic campaign. I was the teacher of homiletics at our Bible school, and the campaign was taking place in the chapel at the Bible school.

I prepared seven sermons on the Good Samaritan, all taken from the one passage. In each, I spiritualized the various aspects of the story. But the point Jesus was making is, "Now, you go and do the same thing."

When you find someone in need, you help him. But in all of my preaching about the parable I said nothing about that.

Paul didn't preach Christ as I did when I analyzed the story of the Good Samaritan. He didn't present the Christ of the Gospels. He was more interested in the eternal, glorious Christ of the present.

When Jesus comes to our churches, He should be the living, glorified Jesus who is present in our midst today. He is the living head of the church. And He has a great deal to say to us when we are ready to listen.

3

The New Covenant Is the Spirit

Paul was on board a ship bound for Rome. He had appealed to the court of Caesar and was traveling as a prisoner to be tried. A tremendous storm came up. It had been cloudy for many days, and because they couldn't see the stars they got lost. As the storm worsened, they despaired. They were weeping and losing all hope of life.

But not Paul. He was singing, even though the ship was sinking.

"How can you sing?" they asked him.

Paul said, "Don't worry. Come on, have something to eat. Be of good cheer."

"How can we be of good cheer?"

"Last night I was talking with the Lord and He told me that the ship is going to sink, but we are all going to be saved. There must be an island around here, and we will be cast on it alive."

Notice, he didn't say to them, "Be of good cheer. Read Psalm 23."

No, he said, "The Lord told me that the ship will sink, and we are all going to be saved."

Paul had the latest ABC news, direct from heaven. He had a personal relationship with Jesus Christ that meant that he didn't have to turn to Psalm 23 to know that he was going to be all right.

A person in whom Christ lives gets up-to-the-minute news. He sees the Lord doing wonderful things continually. He doesn't have to read the newspaper all the time to see the news of what happened yesterday. The newscaster lives within him.

I say this to illustrate a point. Actually, I have a great respect for the Bible, because everything which belongs to Jesus is always a blessing. There is a sense in which it is never old. But the Gospels are only a starting point in a relationship with Jesus, because He still is alive today. The history of His life is not yet finished.

The first time I read the whole of the New Testament I was a little boy; I think I was seven or eight years old. When I got to the last chapter of the book of Acts I was frustrated.

"Where is the rest?" I wanted to know.

The story of Acts finishes where Paul is in the house of arrest. I was disappointed with the ending. I wanted to keep on reading the rest of the story. Of course, that book will always be unfinished, because the Lord is still alive and you can't finish a book about a person who is still alive. How can you finish a biography of a living person?

So Paul says, "Too much consciousness of Christ in the flesh can be a hindrance in knowing Him today as the living person that He is."

This is a problem for us evangelical Christian people. It is hard for us to know the present-day Lord Jesus Christ because we have made an idol of the story of His 33 years on earth almost 2,000 years ago.

Now a knowledge of Christ in the flesh is good. I am not saying anything against it. And I don't think Paul was speaking against it when he said that he was no longer concerned about knowing Christ after the flesh. To know Him in the flesh is good providing you go on knowing Him.

But for Paul, he preferred to know Christ as He is. I have to say that I would prefer to miss a knowledge of Christ in the flesh rather than to miss knowing Him as He is now. Of course, we don't need to miss one or the other; we can have both.

A knowledge of the historical Jesus is static, so it doesn't generate growth. But to know the present-day Lord, that is dynamic. You know Him, and you go on knowing Him all the more. You know Him better today than yesterday.

When I talk about knowing Him, I am not referring to knowing more of the Bible. I have seen people studying the Bible continually in seminary, but they didn't grow one bit spiritually. Others, on the other hand, did grow.

The fact that you read the Bible is not in itself a guarantee that you will grow spiritually.

There are great theologians who know the Bible can help, but it is not a guarantee. But if you know the Bible and you also know the present-day Lord Jesus Christ, the Bible can be a great help.

In the days of the primitive church, the living body of believers spread around the world. They didn't have the New Testament yet. They had to rely solely on the living Christ. They had to depend on Jesus alone.

My concern today is that perhaps we put too much emphasis on our books about the Bible, on the written story of Jesus in the flesh. So much so that we don't need the present-day Lord.

Sometimes I think that we might as well tell Him, "Don't worry, Lord. We have all the sermons You preached when You were on earth 2,000 years ago. We can also repeat the stories of the miracles You performed. Stay in heaven. We really don't need You here."

In the book of Philippians we saw a picture of Christ in His poorest form, made of no reputation, in the form of a servant.

It is a wonderful picture, because the poverty of God is richer than man's finest achievements, the weakness of God is far stronger than man's greatest strength, and the craziest things of God are wiser than the wisest of men. But Jesus' time on earth was still our Lord at His poorest.

In II Corinthians 5:16, Paul explains that the key to spiritual growth is to know Christ as He is now, and not as He was in the flesh. So what is He like now?

Then there is Hebrews 10:19-22, "We have confidence to enter the holy place by the blood of Jesus, by a new and living way which He inaugurated for us through the veil, that is, through His flesh."

The writer is implying that the body of Jesus is a veil. I would have to agree, because that body has hidden the eternal glory of Jesus Christ.

Behind that body the eternal Immanuel, God with us, lay hidden.

Only at times did Jesus show His glory through the veil. One of those occasions was on that mount of transfiguration. As the apostles were looking at Jesus, His flesh and garments could not contain the light.

At the end of His life as He was praying alone in the garden, Jesus said, "Father, give Me again the glory that I had with You before the ages." So the flesh of Jesus was a veil in which this eternally glorious being, the creator of all things, was hidden.

To know the bearded and sandaled One was not really to know Christ. He was hidden behind that body. So the writer of Hebrews exhorts us to go through the veil of His flesh to know Him in spirit.

Of course, the writer had the Old Testament tabernacle in mind.

You remember that the tabernacle had an outer court, then the holy place inside the outer court, and then inside of the holy place was the holiest of all. The holiest lay beyond the veil of the temple. It was a very thick veil, and it was kept closed. Only the high priest got to go within it, and then but once a year. The other priests got to see the outside of the veil, but they never saw within. They ministered in the holy place, but never in the holiest.

But when Jesus died on the cross, the Bible says that the veil of the temple rent in two.

Can you imagine the shock this would be to a priest who might have been ministering in the holy place at the time, perhaps offering frankincense to God? Suddenly, the veil is rent in two and the way into the holiest is open. The priest got to see inside the very holiest.

The real veil that was being rent that day was the body of Christ.

Jesus died for many reasons, but one of them was to finish with that veil. He died to do away with the body of flesh that had hidden His eternal being, His glorious state. So when He died on the cross, the beard and sandals came to an abrupt end. This picture of Jesus had to disappear from the view of the disciples in order to make way for the real Christ who was hidden within that body of flesh.

The author of Hebrews appeals to us to go through the holy place into the holiest—to go beyond the Christ of the Gospels and know Him in the Spirit. We are to worship Him today not in the flesh, but in spirit and in truth.

No wonder the writer had to complain to the Hebrews about their lack of spiritual growth.

They were stuck on the wrong side of the veil. He had to urge them to go on to perfection. And one of the key things they had to do in order to grow was to go through the veil.

When the veil was rent in two in the temple, the Jews quickly sewed it back together again. They closed off the holiest from view. It seems that the church also has sewn the veil back together, and once again we find ourselves on the outside of the veil.

For many years I knew the veil by heart.

The Samaritan woman, the ten lepers, blind Bartimaeus— you tell me the first word, and I'll tell you the rest. I knew it all by heart. I had been hearing the same words since birth. All of my ministry was on the outside of the veil. I was forever preaching about the Samaritan woman, Zacchaeus, and the different events of Jesus' earthly ministry.

One day I saw a little hole in the veil. And I said, "Lord, how come we are still preaching about Your cursing of the fig tree? What would Your angels say if they came to a service, and they saw that the Lord of glory was still cursing a fig tree? Lord, I thank You for cursing a fig tree, but I want to begin ministering on the other side of the veil."

The reason for our lack of spiritual growth in the church is that we have sewn up the veil. Concepts and doctrines concerning the Christ who lived nearly 2,000 years ago are static. They are not alive, so they cannot produce growth; only that which is alive can give growth.

We are more historically-centered than we are Christ-centered.

We have pledged allegiance to the doctrine of a historical Jesus instead of to a living person. That is why we have so many divisions. We all claim to have the truth, but we have different doctrines, even though we don't have different Christs.

If we were Christ-centered, so that Christ would be a living person to us, the actual head of the church, we all would be one. But the head of our church is our set of rules and doctrines about the historical Jesus, so we all are divided.

When we turn to Jesus, unity comes. When a person comes to Jesus, He is the same Jesus of the Catholics, and the same Jesus of the Protestants. Christ is one, not many. But when we turn to our set of rules and doctrines, we are divided.

We have to understand the difference between the old covenant and the new covenant. Paul describes the believer as an "epistle of Christ...written not with ink but with the Spirit of the living God; not in tables of stone but in fleshly tables of the heart" (II Corinthians 3:3).

The old covenant is the Ten Commandments, which were engraved on tablets of stone. But the new covenant is Christ

Himself living within the heart of the believer. It is a totally different kind of covenant! The subjects of the kingdom of God are ruled not by an external law but by the internal government of the King Himself.

Paul went on to say, "Who also has made us able ministers of the new covenant, not of the letter, but of the Spirit; for the letter kills, but the Spirit gives life" (verse 6).

What did Paul mean by the Spirit?

Many believers imagine that the Old Testament is letter and the New Testament is Spirit. Or they think that the new covenant is a more spiritual version of the old law—the law plus the Sermon on the Mount. But all of these are letter!

According to Paul, the new covenant is not a written law, either of the Old Testament or of the New Testament. It is not a spiritual interpretation of the Ten Commandments. Neither is it the Sermon on the Mount. The new covenant is not a written law at all, but it is the Spirit.

So Paul went on to explain, "Now the Lord is that Spirit; and where the Spirit of the Lord is, there is liberty" (II Corinthians 3:17). The new covenant is an agreement God made to come and live within us personally in order to fulfill His will!

The old covenant is letter, the new covenant is Spirit.

The Lord Himself is the Spirit, and He lives within us. To be in the kingdom of God is to be joined to the King so that He rules you from within the new heart.

We can use the Gospels or any part of the New Testament in the same way people use the Old Testament. Actually, it is just the same way the Muslims use the Koran.

We read the Book, then we try to live by it. We see what our founder did, and we try to copy Him. That makes us another religion, like every other religion.

But the new covenant is not a religion!

We have a living Founder, who is alive today. He lives within us, and He in us is the law by which we live. His life is duplicated in us because we have been united with Him, made one spirit with Him (I Corinthians 6:17). That is why Paul could say, "For me to live is Christ." Paul's life was not under his own rule, it was under the control of Christ.

The old covenant is described as a ministry of death. It was a glorious covenant because it contained many beautiful laws. But it ministered death to those who tried to keep those laws because they couldn't do it. For that reason Paul called the old covenant "the ministration of condemnation."

When Moses was given the old covenant he "put a veil over his face, that the children of Israel could not steadfastly look to the end of that which is abolished, but their minds were blinded; for until this day remains the same veil untaken away in the reading of the Old Testament; which veil is done away in Christ. But even to this day, when Moses is read, the veil is upon their heart. Nevertheless, when it shall turn to the Lord, the veil shall be taken away" (verses 13-16).

The people who lived under the covenant had a veil over their hearts.

And I have to say with sorrow, but also with hope, that for many years I too read the Bible with a thick veil on my heart. I was no better off than the people in Old Testament times because of the veil.

I saw the letter and nothing else. I didn't see the Spirit. So the letter was like a veil. I couldn't see God's intention behind the letter. I saw just the lifeless demands of the law—demands that no one has ever been able to fulfill.

Now I understand why Paul called the old covenant, condemnation and death. I tried to live by the law, and I taught others to live by it. But we always felt like failures. We could never do it! So we felt condemned, and we lived with a continual feeling of guilt.

A great many believers are terribly discouraged with trying to live the Christian life because they have the old and the new covenants mixed up. They know that under the new covenant we are not under the law, but they still try to live according to the law. When they find they can't do it, they feel condemned.

Our churches are full of condemned Christians. A lot of us had learned to wear a mask so that we appeared to be doing all right. But behind those masks there were feelings of failure and discouragement. Many believers are in despair because they can't do what they believe they are supposed to do.

It makes me sad to see so many people trying to live the Christian life but finding that they are unable to.

But it also gives me hope. Yes, hope! Now that may seem like a paradox. But in my own life it was only when I came to the end of self-effort—when I saw that I couldn't do all the things Christians are supposed to do—that I gave up and turned to the Lord.

When a man turns to the Lord, the veil is taken away. When we stop trying to do it ourselves and rest in Jesus, trusting Him in us to live the Christian life, we no longer are blinded by the veil. We get ourselves in focus and see clearly.

What do we see when the veil is removed?

I want you to listen very carefully to what Paul said. It is an astounding revelation! If you once can see this, your whole life will be transformed.

When Moses came down from Mt. Sinai after being face-to-face with God for 40 days, his face shone. Some of God's glory may have penetrated his skin so that light actually radiated from his face! It must have been a tremendous sight to see him shine with the glory of God!

But Moses knew that the glory was going to fade away, so he put a veil over his face. Why did he cover himself with a veil? Because he understood people and their reactions, so he was very wise.

If he had come back with the glory shining from him, people would have seen him and said, "Oh, Moses is such a man of God!"

They would have practically worshiped him. But then, when the glory later faded, they would have said, "He lost the anointing!"

I don't know how long the glory lasted. Let's suppose it lasted one month. For the first week it shone brightly. How the people would have revered Moses! The second week, it shone a little less; the third week, less still; until by the end of the fourth week it was gone. What would people have thought of Moses?

We do this with our pastors.

The pastor preaches beautifully, he visits the people and shows a tremendous love for them, and the people praise him. "Oh, pastor, we are so glad to have you here...your ministry is so anointed!"

But then the pastor goes through a difficult time. His preaching doesn't seem so inspired any more. He is not as warm as he used to be when he visits with people.

"He is not like he used to be," people start to say. "He has lost his anointing!"

Now, all of this is a type of the old covenant.

When people live under the law, obeying the letter, they may go along quite well for a time. They discipline themselves and put their lives in order, so that they actually look very holy.

For instance, someone comes along to the meetings and he testifies, "Brothers and sisters, I had a tremendous experience with the Lord. He has delivered me from drugs."

This brother now looks very holy. He is doing all of the right things, so he is accepted by everyone as being very spiritual. He has the glory!

After two or three weeks, he is again in the park, smoking pot. Christ didn't deliver him from drugs at all! Actually, had we been wise we would have put a veil over his face so that nobody knew he quit smoking. The glory he had manifested was simply that of the law, and it quickly faded because the holiness of the letter is usually transitory.

After pointing to the fading glory of the law's temporary holiness, Paul goes on to show that the glory of Christ is very different. "But we all, with unveiled face beholding as in a mirror the glory of Lord, are changed into the same image from glory to glory, even as by the Spirit of the Lord" (verse 18).

Instead of fading, the glory of Christ in a person's life increases from glory to glory.

The reason is simple. It is not an outer holiness that consists of conforming to what others expect of us as Christians. It is an inner holiness that springs up spontaneously, effortlessly, naturally from our core.

The old heart that was in every one of us at birth has been replaced. We have a new heart. The old man tried to be holy, but he couldn't keep it up because his heart was not holy, so the glory quickly faded. But the new man has a heart which is holy, so it is natural for him to live righteously.

The heart is our command-center, like Houston, Texas. In our old life, the one seated within us at the command-center was the god of this world. He was lord of our lives, so that sin ruled us (Ephesians 2:2; Romans 6:20).

But when our hearts turned to the Lord, Satan was ousted from his throne and his internal rule over our lives ceased. In his place, Christ Jesus came to live and reign. He is at our command-center, so that we are under the government of the kingdom of God. He gave each of us a new heart.

In the new covenant, there is no veil. We can look steadfastly at the glory of Christ without a veil to cover it. The veil was done away at the cross, so we are unveiled and He is unveiled.

Now, where do we see this unveiled glory of Christ? Where do we look for it?

Listen to Paul's words, "But we all, with unveiled face beholding as in a mirror the glory of the Lord...." If you remove the veil from your face and look in a mirror, you will see the glory of the Lord! In other words, when you remove the veil of the law from your life and look into a mirror to see who you really are, you will behold the glory of Christ in your own face.

The person who is joined to the Lord under the new covenant is "one spirit" with Him (I Corinthians 6:17). Two have been joined as one. So when we look at ourselves without the veil of the old covenant, we see an expression of Jesus Christ! Hallelujah!

Which Christ do we see?

The present-day Lord, the One who is no longer veiled in flesh. Not the bearded and sandaled One, but the Christ who is joined with us as one spirit and who is our life at this present moment in the 20th century.

That is why we read in Romans 5:10, "For if, when we were enemies, we were reconciled to God by the death of His Son, much more, being reconciled, we shall be saved *by His life.*"

The death of Jesus—the shedding of His blood at Calvary—made possible our forgiveness and justification. Through it we are told that there is "no charge to answer" on the day of judgment.

But the blood of Jesus doesn't empower us to live a saved life. It is by the present-day *life* of Christ that we experience salvation as a dynamic reality.

Salvation is not a present God gives us like a gift wrapped up nicely in a package, so that we can put it on a shelf and look at it. It is not a "thing." Salvation is a life! It is to walk in a particular way, to experience a certain quality of life.

That is why Paul also said, "Work out your own salvation with fear and trembling."

To work out our salvation is to walk as a saved person, to live a saved life. It is to experience the fact of salvation on a day-by-day basis. It is to live from the new heart, to manifest the new creation that we are in Christ.

And how do we work out our salvation? How do we live the saved life?

"For it is God who works in you, both to will and to do of His good pleasure" (Philippians 2:12-13). Christ is our life! He is the One who impells us to do the will of God and empowers us to carry it out. It is He who generates the life in us because we are one with Him.

Paul explained: "For you are the temple of the living God; as God has said, I will dwell in them, and walk in them; and I will be their God, and they shall be my people" (II Corinthians 6:16).

When we live our ordinary, everyday life, God promises that He will live through us. We are vessels to contain Him. He moves us, urges us, motivates us to do His will, so that we can say with Paul that it is no longer we who are living but Christ who lives in us (Galatians 2:20).

Jesus said, "Lo, I am with you always."

This is what the primitive church understood. They had no New Testament, not even the Old Testament; they didn't have copies of the Old Testament at home to read. They just had Jesus Christ.

So they said, "Jesus Christ heals you. Come on, get up."

We say, "Read books about healing." This is because we have a theological approach based on books and meditation, instead of on life. They had the living Person; we have only a concept.

The record of the primitive church was, "And they went forth, and preached everywhere, the Lord working with them, and confirming the word with signs following" (Mark 16:20).

We sing, "I'll never walk alone." We are at least being honest. We don't go alone. We go with the Bible under our arm.

But in the primitive church, they went with the Lord. He dwelt in them and walked in them; He was their life, not just a concept. That is why they moved in such great power.

I recommend that you read the Gospels all over again. Then study the veil.

After you have studied the veil, so that you are sure you understand it, pull it aside and take a look at the ascended Christ who is alive in you today. Look at yourself in a mirror, without a veil of the old covenant law—forgetting the bearded and sandaled One—and see the present-day Christ in action through you at this very instant.

"Lord, there You are, inside of me all this time!"

"Yes, here I am."

Then start to fellowship with Him. Start to have His point of view on all matters affecting your life.

Stop trying to copy the Jesus of nearly 2,000 years ago, and let the living Christ flow through your character. Begin to see His angle on things, and to think with His mind.

"Where the Spirit of the Lord is, there is liberty." Not liberty for license or to turn the benches upside down and to make a lot of noise. But liberty from the bondage of law—liberty from the old covenant. Liberty to be the unique expression of Christ that He created you to be.

Christ is alive today!

Look at yourself in a mirror. Get yourself in focus—discover who you are. You are an expression of the glorified, eternal Christ who lives within you. Begin to believe that about yourself and you will start to experience His life as a daily reality.

4

Wherever We Are, Christ Is

The disciples in Jesus' day had a problem.

They were continually seeking a physical manifestation of the kingdom of God. Jesus had to tell them repeatedly that the kingdom was different from what they pictured.

Today we have the same problem, so I want to stress just one point in this chapter: the kingdom of God is in us.

Don't look for it around you some place because you will not find it there. It is within you.

Paul prayed for the people of God in his day, "That He would grant you, according to the riches of His glory, to be strengthened with might by His Spirit in the inner man; that Christ may dwell in your hearts by faith" (Ephesians 3:16-17).

I want you to notice what he asked. He didn't say, "I ask that you might have nice meetings." No, he asked that our inner man be strengthened, and that Christ may dwell in our hearts by faith.

Where does Christ live?

In our hearts, by faith. That is what it means to be in the kingdom of God. Jesus is the King, and He comes to live within us. We are joined to Him in spirit so that He rules our hearts. We are subject to His government in our lives, and He is our Lord. This is the kingdom of God.

Paul went on to say, "That you may be filled with all the

fullness of God." To be filled is to have Him inside you; just as the water in a full glass is inside the glass, not on the outside.

"Filled with all the fullness of God."
"Paul, do you know what you are saying?"
"Yes, Sir, I know!"

Then he said, "Now unto Him who is able to do exceedingly abundantly above all that we ask or think, according to the power that works in us."

Where does His power work? It works in us.

Paul's message was very simple. It was very down-to-earth, and applied to everyday life. In our theologies we become too idealistic and try to scale the peaks of high mountains. But Paul starts where we are, with the little things of life. And if we are faithful in the little things, the Lord will give us the bigger things.

His Gospel was really good news because it concerned how to live. It was about living today, and tomorrow—the ordinary, everyday life that each of us must lead. He summed it up in one clear statement: "Christ in you, the hope of glory" (Colossians 1:27). This is what the new covenant is about.

Essentially, the difference between the old and new covenants is that the old covenant worked outside of people, whereas the new works within.

With the old covenant, they had to read it in a book and then try to do it.

But the new covenant is, "I will put My law in their inward parts, and write it in their hearts, and will be their God, and they shall be My people" (Jeremiah 31:33). The law is internalized, like a built-in guidance system.

Ezekiel expressed it this way: "A new heart also will I give you, and a new spirit will I put within you; and I will take away the stony heart out of your flesh, and I will give you an heart of flesh. And I will put My Spirit within you, and cause you to walk in My statutes, and you shall keep My ordinances, and do them" (Ezekiel 36:26-27).

We don't have to try to do the new covenant; God causes us to do it from within. It is an internal urge. The Spirit is in us, in the new heart, and impells us to walk God's way.

Jesus expressed it very clearly to His disciples. The Spirit "dwells with you," He told them, "and shall be in you." In you! From Pentecost on, the Spirit is within.

In the Old Testament, they spoke more usually of anointing rather than filling. This was because the Spirit moved upon people from outside to accomplish His purposes. He only visited people. So with the old covenant, the term was anointing.

Now in the new covenant it is not a visit. He comes with all His luggage, to stay, to abide. So in the new covenant we speak of filling more than anointing. He is inside of us.

Jesus made a remarkable statement at the Feast of Tabernacles.

All the people were in Jerusalem participating in this great religious celebration. He went up into the temple and announced to them all, "If any man thirst, let him come unto Me, and drink. He who believes on Me, as the Scripture has said, out of his heart shall flow rivers of living water" (John 7:37-39).

Where does the Spirit come from? Not from outside, but from within the believer! He is in us. This is the new covenant—Christ in us the hope of glory.

We don't need to study to learn how to seek the Lord. We do not have to try to pull Him down from heaven to come and anoint us. He has come to dwell in us through the Spirit, and He seeks to flow out through us. We need to learn how to release what we already have within us.

This is a completely different approach from the attitude many of us have had. We have been trying to seek God, trying to get fresh outpourings of the Spirit from up in heaven. But the Bible presents Christ in us not as a goal to be attained, but as a fact to be realized.

When we continue to think of Christ as being outside of us

and needing to come and fill us, we are denying what the Bible says. We are making the Bible into a lie, because the fact of Christ in us is the greatest and clearest promise of the Holy Scriptures.

Now, we have to be sure that this has really happened to us, that He is within us. But once we have Him within us, He does not have to come into us again. We just need to believe that He is there in all His fullness.

So Jesus said that rivers of living water would flow out of us. Not into us, but out of us.

So to the Samaritan woman He said, "Whosoever drinks of the water that I shall give him shall never thirst, but the water that I shall give him shall be in him a well of water springing up into everlasting life" (John 4:14). The water springs up within and flows out of us.

Paul asked the Corinthians, "Do you not know that your body is the temple of the Holy Spirit who is in you, whom you have of God, and you are not your own?" (I Corinthians 6:19). Again, we see that the Spirit of God is in us. He has taken up residence.

To the Romans, Paul said the same thing. Those who are led by the Spirit of Christ are the sons of God, and if anyone doesn't have the Spirit of Christ he is none of His—he is not a Christian. So we don't have to try to get the Spirit of God. We have the Spirit, and He leads us from within.

That the Spirit is in us is clear from many statements of Scripture. It also is clear from some of the symbols that are used in the Bible. Consider the symbol of the tabernacle or temple.

When the old covenant tabernacle and Solomon's temple were inaugurated, God came down as a flame of fire over the tabernacle and over the temple. He said, "I will abide here; I will live here." He came upon the building.

But on the day of Pentecost, something different happened. God also came with fire to inaugurate the new building, but in this case the building is us.

Jesus said, "Destroy this temple and in three days I will raise it up." This was heresy to those listening. The building had taken years and years to build, and He claimed to be able to build a new temple in three days!

Of course, He was talking about a different kind of temple that would replace the building. He was talking of His body. It takes more than three days to build an earthly temple, but in three days His body was raised up. And this was a symbol of the new temple which you and I form.

I ask myself why it is that we continue to call physical buildings the church. I wonder if we have ever really realized that we are the temple today?

Why do we call a building the church?

Words are symbols of ideas. And though people know that the building is not the church, they still say, "I am going to church."

But that is a wrong idea. We never can go to church because we are the church. The church is not the building at all. I wonder if we do not fail to function as the church all week long because we persist in saying words that give us a concept of the church as somewhere we have to go.

Jesus said, "Where two or three are gathered together in My name, there I am in the midst of them." What does that make us think of? We imagine the church meeting. We think of people coming together to church.

That is not what Jesus meant. He never said, "Where there is a piano and an organ, and two flags, there I am in the midst of them." He said two or three people.

When I wake up in the morning I ask, "Martha, are you there?"

She says, "Yes, Johnny."

We are two, and we both have Christ. We both believe in Him, and we both trust Him. So we are the church. At that particular moment, the church is in bed.

Then we go to the breakfast table, where David joins us, and then Robert John. Soon we are six because our two daughters also arrive. The church is having breakfast. This is the building that Jesus said He would build in three days.

We need to stress what the church really is. We know it in our heads, but we don't know it in our hearts, and so we don't live accordingly.

One of the greatest problems in the church is that we know these things but we don't do them. We don't need a concept, but life. We need to live as we believe.

So on the day of Pentecost when this new building was inaugurated we find that the fire came just as it came upon the tabernacle and the temple. And what did it come upon? The building or the people? It came upon the people. It did not come upon the roof of the building, it came upon the people, because from that day on Christ was going to dwell in those people as He formerly dwelt in the temple.

When we believe in Jesus Christ, He comes to dwell within us.

We pray, "Thy kingdom come." His kingdom comes to our hearts. He enters into us and becomes one with us so that He can rule our lives from our command-center, the new heart.

Where is the risen Lord?

Perhaps you think of Him as beyond the clouds, maybe even beyond the stars. But according to Scripture, where is He? Here, within us. He has come to make His abode with us, to take up residence in us, to eat and drink with us. He shares our everyday, ordinary lives with us—all of the things that we do throughout the day and night.

People think that to live a spiritual life is to live a life that is not normal. They think it is to go to meetings in the church building, or to spend a great deal of time locked away in a room studying the Bible or on their knees. To be spiritual is thought of as something different from ordinary life.

No, to be spiritual is to live the whole time in Jesus. It is to be in union with Him—to be one with Him—and to let Him guide you in all of the things that you do. So you live a normal life, but it is all under the control of Jesus Christ. That is what it is to live in the kingdom of God—to live a full, whole physical life under the internal direction of the King.

This is what Paul was referring to when he prayed that we might "be strengthened with might by His Spirit in the inner man; that Christ may dwell in your hearts by faith...that you might be filled with all the fullness of God...according to the power that works in us."

Christianity is not an external matter, like religion. It is an "in" thing. And it works by faith. We believe that He is within us. We don't have to depend on outer feelings because we know for a fact that Christ is within us.

Perhaps you are saying to yourself about this time, "But we know that. We didn't pick up this book to waste our time reading what we already know. Tell us something that we don't know."

Do you really know it?

For years, I thought I did. I preached about it, using all of the Scripture passages that talk about Christ in us. Yet I would say to the people, "Brethren open your hearts to the Lord."

You see, I was using all the right words, but I didn't know the life. I had the concept, but not the life!

This may make you laugh, but on one occasion I found myself in a situation in my own church which demonstrates the difference between having a concept and experiencing the life.

There was a song leader in our church and he said, "Let's start the meeting with hymn 224, 'Since Jesus came into my heart.'"

We sang the hymn. Then he announced, "Now let's sing hymn 191, 'Come into my heart, Lord Jesus.'"

What happened between the first hymn and the second? In the first hymn He was there, but in the second He is not there—He has to come!

We were more concept- and doctrine-centered than life-centered.

We had a doctrine that said Christ had to come into our hearts, and that is a perfectly correct doctrine. But we also had a doctrine that says Christ is in our hearts. The trouble is, we got them mixed up.

Now if our doctrines were a reality in our lives, when the pastor says, "Let's sing, 'Come into my heart, Lord Jesus,'" we would answer, "Pastor, if you don't have Him, sing it yourself. But we have Him."

We should be careful what we sing, because many of our songs are old covenant. In those days they were right to sing, "Let us go unto the mountain of the Lord, and to the house of our God." The mountain of the Lord was in Jerusalem and the house of God was the temple. But if we don't translate those songs into new covenant, we will get confused.

David sang, "I was glad when they said unto me, Let us go to the house of the Lord."

But in order to sing that psalm, I must translate it. So I simply change it to, "I am glad with those who tell me we are the house of the Lord." This makes it new covenant.

The temple was a shadow. We have the reality. If you sing about going to the house of the Lord, you are thinking of going somewhere, perhaps to the church building. Be careful when you sing the words of the Old Testament, especially the psalms. There are some wonderful psalms, but we need a translation into the new covenant.

I believe that we are suffering the consequences of a tremendous mixing of the old and new covenants. We are trying to live with two husbands at the same time. We want to be married to Mr. Law and to Jesus. That is adultery!

We have died to the law if we are Christians.

Paul tells us this in Romans 7:1-6. We should study that passage carefully, because it is a serious matter to engage in adultery. We no longer are married to the law. We are married to "another" husband—to the ascended Christ.

I was at another service in which the song leader said, "Let us sing, 'There's a river of life flowing out from me.'" Later in the same service they sang, "Cause me to come to Thy river, O Lord." What happened?

We were just singing about a river of life flowing out of us in gushing torrents, and in the next breath we were pleading, "Come and quench the thirsting of my soul." What confusion! No wonder we cannot convince the world of the life that we preach. We are not sure ourselves of what we have and what we don't!

Listen to Jesus' words again: "Whosoever drinks of this water [speaking of the water that sustains physical life] shall thirst again; but whosoever drinks of the water that I shall give him shall *never* thirst, but the water that I shall give him shall be in him a well of water springing up into everlasting life."

When we sing, "Come and quench," we are contradicting Jesus. He talked about rivers of living water welling up within us and flowing out to others, but we speak of being dry and thirsty. Isn't that calling Him a liar?

"Never thirst." That means we are no longer thirsty. "Blessed are those who hunger and thirst, for they shall be filled." But we don't believe the promise that we will be filled, so we continue to speak and to sing about hungering and thirsting for God.

Who was Jesus talking to when He said that those who were hungering and thirsting after righteousness would be filled? No, He was talking to unconverted people who experienced a continual thirst of the soul—who sought the Lord but were unable to know union with Him.

Just as Jesus said in John 6:35, "I am the bread of life; he that comes to Me shall never hunger, and he that believes on Me shall never thirst." He Himself would come to live in them to satisfy the thirst and the hunger of the soul. They would be filled up to all the fullness of God, because He Himself would dwell in them. Isn't that tremendous?

The Scripture says, "Seek and you shall find." But we have got into such a habit of always seeking something outside of us that it is as if we have never found. The truth is, we have found; so we don't need to seek Him any longer. We just need to have our eyes opened to see that He lives within us in all of His fullness and glory!

When we sing incorrect words, we become confused in our theology. We never will grow spiritually if one minute we think we are full and the next minute we are speaking of being empty. We don't know what we are! It is all a conceptual thing and not life.

Christ did not come to bring us a religion, but life. He came to be in a relationship with us. Jesus is a person, and I happen to have that person within me. He came, and He stays here. He said, "If you open to me I will come, and My Father with Me, and we will abide in you."

There is nothing that we need to be more clear on than this. It is vital that we are not messed up on this point. We are the building of God and He is within us. Wherever we are, Christ is. If we are confused on this, we will never grow.

People say to me, "Brother, we have to seek the Lord!"

I tell them, "I never lost Him!"

What do you mean when you say, "Seek the Lord"? That is an old covenant concept. I don't know about you, but I found Him a long time ago, and He happens to be within me.

You know, sometimes when we pray we think of Him as far away. We plead, "Lord, I want to hear Your voice. Lord, Lord, Lord...." We point our fingers outwardly, away from ourselves, as if we were reaching out to Him.

But He says, *"I'm sorry, the higher you point, the further you are away from Me. I am down here."*

When you pray, don't point your fingers outwardly, because He is in you.

Do you know who is *out there*? The god of this world is the one who is out there. But Christ is inside you, and that is the only place you can know Him.

Under the old covenant they said, "Let us lift our hands to the sanctuary and bless the Lord."

But what is the sanctuary today? It is a very different thing from the temple. We are the sanctuary!

I am not saying that we should not raise our arms in worship and praise. If you raise your arms because you are ex-

ploding with an inner joy and you want to express it outwardly, that is wonderful. If gladness is flowing out from you,
then by all means put up your arms.

But if raising your hands gives you a feeling of God being
out there somewhere, then put them down! That is not the
new covenant. If you want to point your hands toward Him,
try pointing your fingers at yourself, because that is where
you will find Him.

We need to be continually conscious of the fact that He is
in us. We have to know beyond a shadow of a doubt that we
have within us all the resources of the One who upholds the
universe.

"Filled to all the fullness of God," as Paul expressed it.

Once we really believe this, so that we no longer are confused as to where He is, then we have to learn how to release
what we have.

5

We Don't Know
What We Have

There are believers in whose lives football has taken the place of Christ. With others, it is money that has taken the place of Christ. They no longer come to church meetings regularly, so those of us who do come to the meetings look with sorrow upon them because they are no longer Christ-centered.

It is very bad when football takes the place of Christ, or money takes the place of Christ. But it is no less tragic when even good things take the place of Christ. The Bible, for instance, or church meetings.

Some people are accustomed to visiting their psychiatrist every week. They say they need that hour with him in order to survive. And for many of us, the church meeting is the same kind of pick-me-up.

Meetings can be wonderful. But my spiritual life is not grounded in meetings. It is grounded in Christ. As we sing in the hymn, "My hope is built on nothing less than Jesus' blood and righteousness. All other ground is sinking sand."

We were considering Paul's prayer for the Ephesians, and we were seeing that his desire was that we might be strengthened with might in our inner man. Now our meetings can be a help in strengthening us in our inner man, or they can be the greatest single hindrance of all. It depends on whether we are meeting-centered or Christ-centered.

"But aren't we all Christ-centered?" someone asks.

When I hear some of the things that Christians say, I wonder if we really are Christ-centered. I frequently hear statements that cause me concern. For instance, especially among the Charismatics and Pentecostals I hear, "Brothers, since I came into this place I felt the presence of the Lord."

So I ask, "And where was the Lord before you came into this place?"

Actually, if we did not bring Him with us, He is not here. He is not in the habit of hanging from the ceiling and descending upon people each time there is a meeting. He does not dwell in buildings; He dwells in people.

Christ is not in Vatican City; nor is He in Dallas, Texas; nor in Springfield, Missouri. He doesn't live in places; He lives in the hearts of individuals. If He is in Vatican City, it is because He is in the heart of the Pope, not because He is in the building.

If Christ is at the meeting when you go there, it is because He is within you. You brought Him with you. So how can you say, "Oh, as soon as I get to the meeting I will feel the presence of the Lord"? That sounds nice, but it is heresy.

Don't confuse emotion with the presence of God.

When people tell me, "I feel the presence of God," I seriously question whether they have any real understanding of the new covenant. Those same people who "feel" the presence of God in meetings also say, "Lord, I am parched"—when they have rivers within them!

Sometimes people say to me, "Brother Ortiz, you are such a spiritual person. You must spend lots of time alone with the Lord. How much time do you spend alone with Him?"

I answer them, "When you leave me, then I will be alone with Him."

You see, I am with Him all day. He is in me, and I am one with Him; so I have no choice but to be with Him continually. When I am with other people, I am with Him; and when I am alone, I am with Him.

I would like to say to these people, "What do you mean

when you speak of my being alone with the Lord? Do you think I call Him and say, 'Listen, Lord, next week I will be alone from one until two each afternoon, so You can come and be with me'?"

Perhaps you think that in order to be alone with the Lord you have to go to a mountain somewhere. No, He is with you all the time. You are in relationship with Him, the closest relationship a person could possibly have. He is inside you!

I cannot say, "Listen, Christ, could you please leave us because I have to talk with this person?" He cannot leave me because we are one! He is my life, so how can we become separate even for a moment?

I engage in a continual dialogue with Him. If I have been talking with a person, as he leaves me, I say, "Lord, bless him." It is not a religion, it is a relationship.

Many of us are dying of thirst in the midst of the Amazon river! We have rivers of living water within us, ready to gush out like a torrent, but we don't know it, so we feel thirsty.

You remember the eldest son of the prodigal son's father. When the prodigal came back, the father made a feast. They had a great party, and they killed the fatted calf. The elder brother heard the sound of music and dancing, and he felt left out. When he learned that his brother had returned and there was great feasting, he got mad.

The father came out to see him and said to him, "Come in and join in the party."

"No, no," he said. "I have been with you continually, but you never so much as gave me a little goat to feast on with my friends. And now this rascal comes, and you kill the fatted calf."

The father answered, "Look, you have always been with me and all my things are yours." In other words he was saying to him, "If you didn't kill a goat to have a feast, it is because you are a fool."

He was complaining, yet he had everything he could have wished for. To release the rivers of water that we have within, we simply need to act as if what God says is true.

I like to use illustrations because they give us a clearer picture than theological definitions. One time I asked one of my deacons to help me illustrate the new covenant.

I said to him in the vestry, "Half way through my sermon I am going to ask you for all your money. I am giving you my wallet, filled with money, but no one will know that it is my wallet. When I say to you, 'Brother Smith, give me all the money you have—hand your wallet over to me. I won't return it to you'—I want you to give it to me."

He rushed up and gave it to me. Everyone was amazed.

I showed them how much money there was in the wallet and they said, "It can't be, it can't be!" They wondered what they would have done if I had asked them!

"Thank you," I said, and I put my wallet in my pocket.

The building was full of surprised faces, but the deacon and I knew the secret. Of course, the money was mine. And if he had not given it to me, I could have called the police!

When God asks you to do something, it is because He first has given you the power to do it. So when He asks you to love and you don't, He can call the police! He has given you the ability to love because Christ is in you. "I can do all things through Christ who strengthens me," said Paul.

We have to learn, not how to get more from God, but how to release all that we have. "The love of God is spread abroad," says Paul. Where? "In our hearts." So all the love we need is there.

Don't say, "Lord, give me more love so that I can love my brother."

If you don't love your brother, it isn't because you don't have enough love. All the love you need is within you. You don't need more love. You need to know how to release the flow of love that is within.

God never commands us to do something we cannot do.
He never will ask you to do something He has not given you
the ability to do. This is His promise under the new covenant.
"I will *cause* you to walk in My ways."

You recall the incident when Peter and John were going to
the temple and they saw a lame man laid at the gate Beautiful.

They didn't point to the man and tell him, "You need to
come to our campaign so that we can teach you four steps to
healing. If you will learn them and believe them, you can be
healed."

No, they said, "What we have, we give."

Once I invited an evangelist to preach in my church. At the
close of the service he said, "If you don't have faith, don't
come to the throne."

I said to him, "Look, if we had faith, we wouldn't have
needed to invite you here. We wanted to hear you because we
believe you have more faith than us."

Peter and John didn't ask the man to do something. They
conferred upon him what they already had. It was just the rivers
of water flowing spontaneously out of them. They *knew* what
they had. The problem is, we don't know what we have.

We say, "Oh, please heal someone, Lord!"

Then we turn to the individual and we say, "Now, move
your leg."

We should say, "What we have, we give."

I am not trying to ridicule what we do. Let's keep on doing it
if it helps people in the meantime. Praise the Lord for what He
already has given us. But I am waiting for more, for the full operation of the new covenant, the unlimited outpouring of Christ
in us. And I believe we are discovering how it can happen.

What does it mean to live in the Spirit?

To live in the Spirit and to walk in the Spirit is to be continually conscious of the presence of Christ in you. That's all it is!

"What? That's too simple!"

Many books have been written about walking in the Spirit.

Some of them are very good. But most of those books deal with all of the things we need to unlearn, not what we need to learn in order to live in the Spirit. They are directed at Christians who are in error.

What about the new convert? Does he need to read all of Watchman Nee's books in order to be able to live in the Spirit? If he does, then life in the Spirit becomes something difficult because only a certain kind of people can read all of those books.

Life in the Spirit should be the easiest thing you can imagine. The things of the kingdom of God are easy, simple. That is why Jesus said that in order to understand the life of the kingdom we have to forget how intelligent we are and become like children.

Today, especially, we are intelligent people because we have a great deal of education. I believe that there are many things concerning the Gospel that we do not understand—not because they are difficult, but because they are too easy and don't appeal to us.

One of the leaders in our church is an economist. He is a doctor of economic science and professor of mathematics at the university.

While I was preaching one morning I asked, "How much is two plus two?"

At first he smiled at me, because the answer was obvious. But I didn't smile back. I kept a very serious, puzzled look on my face. So he, too, became serious. He began to do all the equations he could think of with the number two.

I stayed silent, and the whole congregation became intent. After a little while he said, "I don't know, pastor."

I said, "Thank you."

There was a little child in the next row. So I said to the child, "How much is two plus two?"

"Four." The answer came right back without delay.

You see, it was too easy for the doctor of economic science. He could not believe that I could ask him such a simple question as how much is two plus two. And because it was so easy he began to look for something more complicated in my question.

Jesus said, "I thank you, O Father, Lord of heaven and earth, because You have hidden these things from the wise and prudent, and have revealed them unto babes." If we understand what He meant—that life in the kingdom of God is a very simple thing—we have discovered the key to living in continual joy and peace.

The things of the Lord have to be very simple if they are for the poor and uneducated. If they are not simple, they may be meant for some theologian in England or Germany, but they are not for me.

To walk in the Spirit is more simple than you can imagine.

You don't need to read any books. Even this one. Actually, the more you read, the more confused you will become until you really understand the simplicity of the Gospel. That is why I never give books to new converts.

We need to have the eyes of our hearts opened to see that because Christ is in us, we have all that is needful for walking in the Spirit. If we once can see that He in us is everything, and that we are joined as one with Him so that we are continually in His presence, life becomes very easy.

Suppose that you are a sister in my church and I see you at the corner of the street. I say to myself, "Oh, I am going to say hello to that sister."

So I run after you to try to catch you. But you don't know that it is I, so you keep on walking. And when you realize that someone is coming after you, you start to walk quicker and quicker. Then you run. So I run.

After three blocks, as I am out of breath, I shout, "Sister, it's I...Johnny Ortiz!"

"Oh, Brother Ortiz, what a blessing to see you. Alleluia!" you tell me.

"But listen, I've been trying to catch you for three blocks," I explain, "but you were not conscious that it was I."

Sometimes we do this with Jesus. We treat Him as though He were not here.

You see, we can be talking about Jesus, but in our consciousness we can be far from Him. For instance, when we sing words like, "Come into my heart Lord Jesus," and He is already there.

Do you remember the two disciples who were walking to Emmaus? They were talking about Jesus. And as they did so, He caught up with them and started to join in their conversation. They were talking about Him, but they were completely unconscious of the fact that He was there with them.

"What are you talking about?" He asked.

"You mean you don't know?" they responded in amazement. "Everybody is talking about Jesus Christ. How come they all know but you. Are you a stranger who has just arrived in the city? Don't you even know who He was?"

Even as He began to expound the Scriptures to them concerning Himself, they continued to be unconscious of His presence.

Norway produces the cheapest electricity in the world, so they never think of turning lights off. They keep them on day and night. Their electricity is generated by the many rivers and falls in their country.

The Vikings lived in the same country centuries ago, but they used candles. They didn't use the power that they had available because they were unconscious of its potential.

Paul prayed that we might experience all of the fullness of God according to the power which works *within* us. But we sing, "Come and quench my thirsty soul...." How silly. We are asking for something we already have, all because of a lack of consciousness.

I would like to take hold of God's people and shake them. We need to see how stupid we have been. Somehow we have to change this situation, because the world is waiting for us to wake up, so that we can share with them not a doctrine but a life!

Christ is in us all day long. But we think that He is only in our meetings. So we go to the meetings to feel His presence.

We act as if He were in the ceiling of the church building. When we come in, we imagine that we can pull Him down by our singing. So after we sing two or three of those "nice" songs, He comes down and blesses us—then He goes up again until next Sunday when we return to feel the presence again.

There are people who go from one "nice" meeting to another to experience the presence. But these people are not living by faith; because Paul said that we are to experience Christ dwelling in our hearts by faith, so that we are continually conscious of His presence.

There is a great deal of confusion about what the presence of God is. If the choir sings nicely, the organ plays beautifully, the pianist excells, and the pastor sounds inspired, we say, "Oh, what a sense of God's presence there was today!"

But if the choir lost the tune because the organist didn't come, and the pastor forgot his notes, we say, "Oh, the service really lacked God's presence today."

No. All that we were missing was the presence of the organist, not the presence of God. God's presence has nothing to do with the choir, the organist, the pianist or the pastor. We have Christ's presence within us whether the organist comes or not. It doesn't depend on whether the choir sings nicely or not.

"There's a river of life flowing out from me," we sing. Where does the river come from? Not from the beautiful singing or the atmosphere of the service, but from inside us. We don't need external things in order for the river to flow.

The author of the book of Hebrews says that all of these external things are going to be shaken, and only the unshakeable will remain.

So be careful if you depend on these things for a sense of God's presence. Because those things could be shaken and we could lose the organ and the choir, the building, the pastor and everything else. But Christ always remains.

Don't lean on the shakeable things, lean on the unmovable

kingdom of God which reigns in your heart because Christ lives there. All the other things are just like icing or ornaments.

Thank the Lord for these luxuries that we have—the singing groups, the buildings, the organs and pianos. Thank the Lord that we have the luxury of talented people to come and sing to us. But those things may one day end. The many great ministries, and even your pastor, may cease to function. But Christ in you still will be there.

Did you ever notice that Paul had the same attitude whether he was in the pulpit or in jail?

He could have enjoyed the organ, the piano, the two flags—or jail and stocks. It was all the same to him. He could sing in both places, even when he had 39 lashes on his back.

Why was Paul able to do that?

He spoke of, "The God whom I serve in my spirit." It was not the atmosphere, the building, the organ, the candles that constituted worship for Paul. He worshipped in his spirit, without all of these things. And we, too, need to get used to being without those things so that we can focus our attention on Christ alone, the King who reigns within our spirit.

To walk in the Spirit is to be continually conscious of His presence.

Suppose I were to come and visit you tomorrow. I knock on the door, but nobody opens it. I listen, and I hear noises inside.

"Somebody is in here," I say to myself, "and they don't want to open the door."

I really bang hard on the door, but there is no response.

So I open the door and walk in. And you are there.

"Hello, how are you?"

You don't answer. Instead, you go to the kitchen. So I follow you there.

"I came to visit you," I explain.

You ignore me and begin to peel your potatoes. When you have done that, you go into another room and begin cleaning it.

Again I follow you. You go to the supermarket, and still I

follow after you. You go to the bank, and I also go there with you. But you don't pay any attention to me.

All day I follow you, but you don't even talk to me.

The next day, I come to your house again. I follow you the whole day, and still you ignore me. You act as if you were completely unconscious of my presence.

On Sunday, you come to the services and you see me there. "Oh, Brother Ortiz, how are you? I'm so pleased to see you!"

You act as if you hadn't seen me for a long time.

"What's wrong?" I ask. "I've been with you the whole week!"

That's what we do with Jesus. He is with us all week, but we wait until Sunday to feel His presence. We treat Him as if He weren't with us the whole time. And I have to tell you that this kind of religion is heresy. It is the complete opposite of what the new covenant is all about.

When Jesus comes to church, it is not just to be there for an hour or so on Sunday. It is to enjoy a continual communion with us, every day of the week. When He comes, He never leaves us. We are in church with Him all the time, 24 hours a day.

It is time we became conscious of His presence.

6

Good Morning, Lord Jesus

As a student in Bible school, I was told that to walk in the Spirit I should set aside an hour each morning to pray and read the Bible.

In order to be ready to start my prayers at 6 a.m., I had to get up at 5 a.m. And I did it. Day after day I dragged myself out of bed to pray and study my Bible for an hour.

But one day, I could not do it; I was simply too tired to get up. And throughout that whole day I felt condemned!

The day came when I discovered that if Christ lives in us, we can enjoy a continual dialogue with Him.

At first when I started to have fellowship with Him all day long, I got on my knees at 6 a.m. as usual. The difference was that when I got up off my knees I kept on talking with Him.

One day after I had got up after my morning prayer time, He asked me, *"Why do you kneel down there? Don't you talk with Me all the time, even when you are not kneeling down?"*

It began to dawn on me that when I talked with Jesus all day long, that was a part of real life; it was a meaningful relationship. But praying an hour each morning was not life to me. It was bondage to a religion. I enjoyed my conversation with Jesus all through the day, but my prayer time was a duty.

I believe that a great many people are under bondage to a

religious system in their daily lives because they don't realize that to walk in the Spirit is to be continually conscious of Christ's unending presence within us.

Today I find that I have an attitude of conducting a continual dialogue with Him.

As soon as I wake up in the morning, I stretch and yawn and say, "Good morning, Lord Jesus. How are You?" (I am still in bed, not down on my knees!)

He answers me, "Fine. And you, Johnny?"

"Wonderful," I reply. "I slept so well last night."

"Yes, I saw that."

"Oh, I think I will stay in bed a few more minutes, Lord."

Because He is my Friend He wants my day to go well so He urges me, "Johnny, get up. You know that when you stay in bed, you end up having to rush. Why spoil the morning by rushing? You are awake, aren't you? You can get up in plenty of time."

"Yes, Lord, but...."

"Come on, get up. Perhaps Sunday you can sleep in. But today, get up so that you don't have to rush."

So I get up and I go to the bathroom to take my shower. As I do so, I continue to dialogue with Him.

"Lord," I say, "while I wash myself outside, why don't you wash me inside?"

"You really need it, Johnny!" He tells me.

When I finish my shower He begins to teach me how to be a good husband. As I leave a puddle of water on the bathroom floor He says, "Johnny, dry the floor of the bathroom—there's the mop. And those hairs in the sink, clean them up."

"Lord," I reason, "my wife can get them later. She has more time."

"Do it yourself, Johnny," He commands me. "Come on, I want to teach you to be a good husband."

"Yes, Lord." And I set about cleaning up the mess.

Then He asks, "How do you feel now?"

"Great, Lord." It is a really good feeling to show love to other people.

I go back into the bedroom and I say to myself, "Let's see, which clothes shall I wear today? I will use these grey pants with the blue coat. Oh, but this blue coat is wrinkled. Let's see if this brown coat will do. No, it doesn't fit with the grey pants. I'll have the beige pants."

By this time I have several items of clothing out on the bed, and I am planning to leave them there for my wife to put back.

Again the Lord says to me, "Johnny!"

"What?"

"Hang up those clothes."

"But my wife can do it."

"Do it yourself, Johnny."

"Yes, Lord." So I hang all the clothes back where they came from and the room looks tidy again.

"Now, how do you feel?"

"Great, Lord, really great. Oh, it's time to dash to the office—I'll miss my bus."

I am about to go out the door, neglecting to take a moment to kiss my wife, and the Lord says to me, "Johnny."

"What?"

"You didn't kiss your wife."

"But Lord, it's late."

"Come on, do it—or she will be upset for the rest of the day."

I say to Martha, "Sweetie, bye bye; I'm leaving now." And as I go out the door I stop to kiss her.

"Oh, I thought you were leaving without even giving me a kiss," she tells me, relieved to see that I am not neglecting her.

"Thank you, Jesus," I whisper, grateful that He knows how to show love in all the little ways that are important to a woman.

When people hear me tell about talking with Jesus they ask, "What do you find to say to Him?"

Do you think that Jesus comes into our hearts just to speak to us about baptism or the millennium? Of course not. He wants to teach us how to live—how to be loving husbands and good fathers. So He talks with me all day long, and I talk with Him. We talk about everything.

If we would listen to the way in which many of us pray, we would see that we don't really know Jesus as our best friend.

When you have a friend, you talk with that person by sharing the ordinary things of life. Your vocabulary, your sentences and the themes you discuss are different with a friend than with someone you meet only occasionally. You drop the protocol and you become intimate.

If you have life rather than religion, your relationship with Him will be intimate because you are growing in friendship. What you talk about with Him will be new every day.

I was a single pastor, and Martha was one of the members of my church. One Sunday morning after the service I went outside the church building and there was Martha with a group of girls.

"Martha," I said, "I would like to talk to you in private if possible."

"Do you mean right now?" she asked.

"Well, I think that it would be nice to talk now," I answered.

"Yes, Pastor," she said.

She came to my office and I said, "Sister Martha, I wonder if you have noticed that I feel for you something different than I feel for the other sisters of the church?"

She became pale. "No, Pastor," she stammered, "I didn't notice it."

"Well," I said, "I would like you to start to notice it."

Suppose that after that first Sunday morning when I spoke to Martha about my feelings for her, the next Sunday I had also said, "Sister Martha, I wonder if you have noticed that I feel for you something different than I feel for the other sisters of the church"?

And the next Sunday, and every Sunday after that, "Sister Martha, I wonder if you have noticed...."

She would have screamed, "Shut up!"

We never would have become married and brought up four children, because a relationship cannot develop when we use the same words of protocol.

That was what I said to her the first time only.

Since then we grew in friendship. I don't have to repeat the same things because we talk, we fellowship, and we are in love with one another. A great depth of intimacy has developed between us in which we share everything together.

But listen to the prayers of many people in church services. Year after year they say the same prayers.

"Dear Heavenly Father, we come into Your presence this morning. We thank You for this meeting. We ask You to be with those who couldn't come, we remember the widows, the missionaries...."

The next Sunday, "Lord, thank You for this meeting. We ask You to be with those who couldn't come, we remember the widows, the missionaries...."

How can we always say the same things to the Lord in our prayers?

He must be really bored with all that protocol. Sometimes I think He must ask Himself, "Is that a cassette playing, or is it the person himself?"

God is your Father. Jesus is your brother. He lives within you! He wants to experience a relationship with you, not to listen to your religion.

The church is the bride of Christ; we are in a relationship with a person who is to become our husband. We are in love with Him, and He is our best friend. In one of our hymns we sing, "Friendship with Jesus, fellowship divine." But this has to be our experience.

We also sing, "He lives, He lives, Christ Jesus lives today. He walks with me and He talks with me, along life's narrow way." Is that really your experience? Do you walk and talk with Him in all of life's situations?

I go to the supermarket quite often to do the shopping.

If you are like me, when you go to the supermarket you tend to buy many things that you don't need. When I see something on one of the shelves I say to myself, "I'll get that."

But while I am shopping, Christ is still living within me. So He says to me, "You don't need that, Johnny."

"Thanks, Lord," I tell Him. *You see, He helps me with the shopping. And He will help you if you will listen to His voice.*

Sometimes I hear gossip. "Brother so-and-so, that tremendous preacher...," then out comes some shocking rumor about that brother.

"No!" I say.

"Yes," the person reassures me.

A little while later I am with another brother. "Did you know what happened with so-and-so?"

At that moment a voice speaks within me, "Don't say it."

Before I knew that it was the voice of Jesus, I went ahead and said what I was going to say. Then I felt bad. But I have learned to listen to that voice and obey it. This is what it means to obey the commands of Jesus under the new covenant.

I can't tell you about many of my conversations with Jesus because you would be shocked. Many of you wouldn't believe that I actually talk to Him in the way I do. But when there is a deep friendship between two people, there is a closeness in which you can share everything.

As I am walking back from the supermarket, I see a nice tree and I say, "What a beautiful tree, Lord. Oh, look at those flowers!"

Then a pretty woman passes in front of me. "Wow, what a woman!"

"Johnny!"

"Lord, don't tell me she is not pretty."

"Yes, Johnny, but...."

"When I told You what a nice tree that was, You were glad. When I mentioned the flowers, You also were pleased. Now I say, 'What a beautiful woman,' and You get upset. Lord!"

"But, Johnny, you know what I mean."

Then I admit, "Yes, Lord, I know what You mean."

Someone asks, "Brother Ortiz, do you pray like *that*?"

So I ask them, "What do you think? When I see a nice woman, do you think I say, 'Lord, this is not for You, don't look'?"

You know, there are people who wait until the next evangelistic meeting to make their confessions?

The Lord says, *"Come on, I was right there with you—and you have waited until the meeting to tell it to Me!"*

Jesus is there with us all the time—not just to forgive us our sins, which He also does, but to prevent us from falling. If we had a continual fellowship with Him, holiness would come easily to us.

"Lord, look at that woman," we might say.

"Johnny, be careful."

"Yes, Lord. Thank You for reminding me, but she is beautiful."

He won't forbid me to say that she is beautiful. But because we are talking continually, He keeps me from going any further. Remember, we can lust with our eyes as well as with our bodies.

Perhaps you say, "Brother Ortiz, how do you know that Jesus speaks to you? It can be the flesh that speaks to us, or it can be Satan."

Listen. If we don't know this, then we know nothing; because those who are led by the Spirit, those are the sons of God.

The Lord promised, "I will put My Spirit within you, and cause you to walk in My ways." And Jesus said, "The Spirit of truth will guide you into all truth.... He will teach you all things."

If it isn't as clear as clear can be how He talks to us, His promises are meaningless.

7

Jesus Talks To Us Through Our Consciences

Several years ago I read some books, which contained wonderful truths. But I found a number of points on which I became confused.

The author talked about the spirit, soul and body. The soul and body are the outer man, he explained, and the spirit is the inner man. Christ dwells in our spirit, in the inner man.

As I read about the outer man and the inner man, I began to get upset because I didn't really understand it from a practical point of view.

One day I got so upset that I said, "Lord, I have to know more about this, because if I don't know this, I know nothing."

So I put my head down on the top of my desk and I said, "Lord, I want to find out what is my flesh, what is my soul, and what is my spirit." I didn't have any problem with my flesh. I could touch my physical body. And I knew that my soul is my intelligence, my ability to think and feel.

"But where is my spirit?" I asked myself. I could individualize my body and my psyche, but not my spirit. I couldn't find it.

The soul and the spirit are very close. However, there is a difference between them because the Scripture says that the Word of God parts the soul from the spirit. But the more I tried to understand what is the soul and what is the spirit, the more confused I became.

Another day I said to myself, "I will start the other way. Instead of using the deductive method, I will use the inductive one. I will start from the inside."

So I asked myself, "What is the most inward thing that I am conscious of having?"

Well, the most private, inner part of my being that I knew of was my conscience. I decided to look into the Bible to see what it said about the conscience.

Try it sometime. Make a Bible study of the conscience. You will find that the conscience is the spirit of a man.

God made within us a room for Himself. This room is our conscience. The New Testament uses the words "conscience" and "spirit" interchangeably. For instance, Paul said, "I serve God with a clean conscience." He also said, "The Spirit gives testimony to our conscience."

When I speak of the conscience, everybody knows what I am talking about. But when I say "spirit," it isn't clear what I mean. And if our spirit is our center from which we are to live, it has to be clear to us what it is. So I found that the conscience is our spirit.

Now immediately someone is going to say to me, "Brother Ortiz, you cannot be led by your conscience because everyone's conscience tells him something different."

I said a moment ago that the conscience is a room for God Himself to dwell in. When He is not there, the conscience takes the shape of all the other things we feed it.

If you grow up in a Buddhist country, your conscience takes a Buddhist form and dictates to you Buddhist thinking.

If you are raised in a Catholic family, your conscience is shaped by the Catholic faith. A Catholic brother has no problem with kneeling in front of an image and honoring that image, which is a symbol of a saint, because his conscience allows him to.

Your conscience will always take on the context in which you live. So if you are in a home where you continually are exposed to curse words and stealing as a way of life, you will grow up accepting that as normal.

The conscience is shaped in such a way by our schools today that some children say, "But Daddy, free sex is perfectly normal."

I was riding in a taxi in Buenos Aires one time, and the taxi driver was very talkative.

"I used to have an apartment for my woman," he explained, "and now I cannot afford the apartment any more because of inflation. I don't know what life is coming to with all of the economic problems."

He spent the next ten minutes telling me about the things he did in that apartment. Eventually I said, "Listen, do you think that everybody is like you?"

He looked at me rather curiously and said, "What do you mean?"

"I mean that when I married my wife, that was the first woman I ever knew, and I knew her the first day we were married. I have never been involved with any other women."

He looked at me as if to say, "From which planet are you?" It seemed quite normal to him to have a woman on the side because that is the way his conscience had been shaped.

I was brought up in a Pentecostal church, so my conscience was shaped by the Pentecostal doctrine.

We could not smoke, of course, nor drink; and it was not permissible to listen to the radio. It was considered all right to swim with all your clothes on; but since that would not have been too comfortable and it was sinful to wear a swimming suit, we never swam.

We were not allowed to whistle. So I never learned to whistle. Even today I can't. Had I tried to whistle, my conscience would have accused me because it had been shaped that way. Perhaps you laugh at that. But you also were shaped in some way that is not right.

You may have a Presbyterian conscience, so if you fall into sin you know that you are still going to be saved since you believe in once saved, always saved.

If you are an Arminian, your conscience will tell you that you can fall and be lost, needing to be saved again, every day.

The Bible says that the blood of Jesus will cleanse our conscience from dead works. One day I realized that just as the people of the world need to be cleansed from drug addiction, sexual abuse and all kinds of other sins, I also needed to be cleansed of Pentecostalism.

My conscience was not made for Pentecostalism, just as yours was not made for Presbyterianism or whatever religion you have been involved in. It was made so that Jesus might dwell there. It was created to be indwelt by a Person, not a concept.

From the time I asked Jesus to cleanse me, He went to work on me. The first thing that happened was that I started to love everybody. Before, I did not love Catholics; in fact, I preached against them. When I said, "Jesus, cleanse me," I started to love the Catholics. As a result, they began to receive me.

Jesus talks to us through our conscience.

We are built with a system of communications within us, and the conscience is there to speak to us. Actually, the conscience speaks much more quickly than the mind. Before the mind understands, the conscience already has said, "No!" or "Yes." This is what we call intuition.

When we ask Christ to come into our heart, His Spirit becomes one with our spirit. He takes command of our intuition. So when we are going to criticize somebody, He tells us, "Don't do it."

Someone listening to me says, "What were you going to say about so-and-so, Brother Ortiz?"

And I answer, "Oh, just what a wonderful person he is."

In my heart I say, "Thank You, Lord. Alleluia! I didn't say it." And I feel good inside, because I followed the voice of the Master as He spoke to me through my intuition.

The problem is that we mix our conscience with the mind.

So when the conscience says, "Give a hundred dollars," we pass the order to our office to be approved. We think it over in our mind.

Now my mind tells me, "You already have given a hundred dollars to that person. Don't you remember? He didn't use it properly. Why should you give him a hundred dollars this time? You had better not give him anything."

So I decide not to give him anything, and I quench the Spirit.

To quench the Spirit is not just to tell a person who is speaking in tongues, "Shut up." No, to quench the Spirit is to disobey that inner voice.

We are married to Jesus, our Husband, who lives within us, and He helps us in all of life by speaking to us through our intuition. So if we obey His inner voice we are living in His will. "For all who are being led by the Spirit of God, these are the sons of God" (Romans 8:14). This is what it means to walk in the Spirit—to be led by Christ through our intuition.

On Easter morning, a lady sang that beautiful hymn to which we already referred, "He lives, He lives, Christ Jesus lives today; and He walks with me, and talks with me, along life's narrow way. He lives, He lives, salvation to impart. You ask me how I know He lives? He lives within my heart."

Everybody applauded the beautiful way in which she sang. After the service, another lady came to her and said, "Sister, what did He tell you?"

"What?" said the singer, looking puzzled.

"What did He tell you the last time He talked to you?" the lady persisted.

"What on earth are you talking about?"

"The last time you talked with Him and He talked to you, what did you talk about?"

"Who?" said the singer.

"Jesus. The last time you talked to Him and He talked to you, what did you talk about?"

"What? Me talking to Jesus? You are crazy! Jesus didn't talk to me. Be careful, Sister. If you think that Jesus talks with you, be careful. It could be your flesh, or it could be Satan. People can be misled. We should just read the Bible and follow that."

"But listen, you said, 'and He walks with me and talks with me....' "

"Oh, but that is just a song. He doesn't really talk to me."

"Then why did you sing it?"

"Well, because it's in the hymn book."

No wonder we can't convince unbelievers that Jesus is the way, the truth and the life. If we sing something just because it's in the book, we will never convince anybody.

Once I was in Lincoln Cathedral in England. It is a tremendous building, almost 700 feet long, with an organ in the middle of it. And the English people really know how to do liturgy beautifully. The choir and the ministers were all dressed up in long robes.

I was to offer a prayer during the service. So I thought to myself, "That Cathedral, with all that ceremony...I will do a nice prayer."

When I stood up I said, "O Most High and Holy Father, I come into Your presence this morning...."

About that time He told me, "Johnny, shut up! We have been talking all day long and now you come with this, 'High and Holy Father.'"

I said, "Lord, listen. Let me finish this official prayer, then we will continue our conversation. But I can't stop in the middle of this now that I've started."

"Well, go on,"He said. (He realized that I was in a predicament!)

Jesus is tired of the protocol. All of that "Heavenly Father, O Most High" protocol comes out of the old covenant. But we are Jesus' wife. And I would never say to my wife, "O Heavenly Martha, I come into your presence."

God is hungry for friendship. He wants to seat us on His lap and have us call Him, "Daddy." That is what *Abba* means. "Friendship with Jesus, fellowship divine."

I want to prove to you that God speaks to you.

Take a piece of paper and draw two lines on it so that you divide it into three columns. Draw a line across the top. Above this line put three titles, one on each column. Above the first put, "God said." Above the second put, "I did." Then above the third put, "Result." Do it when you get up in the morning.

So when you take a shower and you get the bathroom floor wet, if God says to you, "Get the mop," put that down in the first column.

Then put down, "I did it."

Under the third column, "Joy and peace."

If God says, "Hang up those coats" while you are getting dressed, write it down.

Then put, "I hung them up."

Under result, "Joy and peace."

Then under "God said" write, "Go back and kiss your wife." In the second column put down, "I didn't."

Result: "No result—consequences."

God said, "Don't say that about your brother." I said it. Result: Unrest.

Don't tell me that you don't know what I am talking about.

You know that the Lord speaks to you like this. The problem is that in our religious system we were taught that the only way God speaks to us is through the Bible. But the Bible tells us what I am telling you. It has all kinds of stories of God speaking to people. And it tells us that He also will speak to us.

When the Spirit tells you, "Clean up the bathroom," you say, "Where does the Bible say I have to clean the bathroom?"

Or when the Spirit tells you, "Give ten dollars to that man," you answer, "The Bible says it's not by works, it's by faith."

If you are all alone, with no telephone close to you, and you have to make a decision, do what that inner voice tells you.

But let me give you a word of advice: You are not independent; you belong to a family of believers. If you think that the Lord is telling you to sell your house and give the money to a ministry, the same Christ in your brothers will tell them the same thing, so ask them for a confirmation. It is a simple matter of safety to check with others with whom you have fellowship and who live by the same inner guidance of the Spirit.

I am not giving you a philosophy; I am giving you something that is life to me. It works. So don't sing, "He lives, He lives, Christ Jesus lives today," because it is in the hymn book. Sing it because you know that He lives within your heart.

You may be able to find all kinds of faults with what I am saying.

We are all human. None of us walks in the Spirit perfectly. But get the heart of my message and begin to hear from the Spirit yourself.

You will make mistakes because we all do. But you will increasingly learn to walk in the will of God as Jesus leads you through the Spirit within.

8

To Lead Is To Live, Not Just Profess

There are lots of people who never come to church. But I have found that many of those who will not come to church would come to Jesus. They are not against Jesus; they are against coming into our church system. We have complicated something that was meant to be simple.

Of course, we who are in it get used to this confusing religious system. But that does not make it right. We on the inside are in the minority. All our rules make it very difficult for those who are on the outside to understand, and they are the majority.

I believe that the things of God are much easier and simpler than we have made them.

Life in the Spirit has to be easy so that the most ordinary person can live it. It has to be natural. It can't be something that you need to read a great many books to understand. Neither can it be something that is frightening us by warning, "Be careful—that could take you into mysticism. That is dangerous."

When we come into God's way of life we are not coming into some strange new thing that is alien to us as human beings. It is the natural way for a human to function. The life of the Spirit is the way God intended all men to live from the very beginning, in harmony with all of the natural laws of the universe. It is very normal.

Abraham is called the father of the faithful—the model of all who are in the Christian way. What kind of relationship did he have with God?

It was a normal relationship, not a religion. It was very natural, very simple.

When Abraham fellowshipped with God he said such things as, *"God, look—You didn't give me any sons. And my heir is going to be one that is born in my house as a slave. Come on, God, do something about it."*

It was a very natural thing for Abraham to talk with God in this way because their relationship was that of two friends. The Scripture says Abraham was the friend of God.

The most complicated thing Abraham did was to make an altar on which to offer sacrifices. Yet it was a spontaneous natural thing for him to do. And where did he build it? He was used to talking with God any place, and when he wanted to give special thanks to God he just did it in his backyard.

In our situation, even the need for an altar has disappeared because Jesus offered one sacrifice forever.

The complicated side of Abraham's fellowship with God was finished at the cross. There are no complications at all for those who are living in the Spirit today. We live the most natural, simple life possible.

A few hundred years after Abraham, the law came. This was the foundation of the Jewish religion. The law seems very complicated to us, and we wonder how a God of simplicity could originate such a complicated system.

But hidden beneath the complications of the law was a very simple way of life. Actually, the only real complications to it were the sacrifices and the temple system. And we can omit all of that because Jesus was the Lamb of God Himself, the perfect sacrifice. So let us look at the teaching of the law.

How simple it was in its essence comes out in Deuteronomy 6:6 where God explained, "And these words, which I am commanding you today, shall be on your heart; and you shall teach them diligently to your sons and shall talk of them when you sit in your house and when you walk by the way and when you lie down and when you rise up. And you shall bind them as a sign on your hand and they shall be as frontals on your forehead. And you shall write them on the doorposts of your house and on your gates.''

This was something that was for the whole of life—it was for everyday living. It affected their homes, their jobs, their walks in the fields, and even what they did in their bedrooms.

"You shall teach My ways diligently," said God. And where were they to teach them?

"In Sunday School?"

No.

"Sunday mornings at ten o'clock?"

No.

Listen: "When you sit in your house, when you walk in the way, when you lie down, and when you get up in the morning." What does that mean?

Always!

You see, even under the law God had in mind a way of life, not a religion. God intended His way to be their life. They were to teach these things to their children. And who was to do the teaching? The father and mother, not the Sunday School teacher. It was not to be a complicated matter, with classes and books and teachers. No, it was to be a part of normal life, passed on by father and mother.

When were they to teach? Continually. Not on Sunday mornings, but all the time.

Today our Sunday School education may be very necessary because in their homes children do not receive what they should be receiving.

Since they are undernourished, we need a hospital to put them in on Sunday mornings. We have to provide them with an oxygen tent and a specialized doctor to give them shots of Bible vitamins because in their homes they are not fed.

We send people to seminaries to prepare them with a Christian education, and the seminaries too are like hospitals. If people were all healthy and never got sick, we would not need hospitals, doctors or universities in which to study about how to cure diseases.

Our systems are all geared to how to cure this and that spiritual ailment because our homes are not functioning as they should. We teach our children how to use a knife and fork, but we don't teach them the Christian life. And I don't mean instructing them in a religious system. I mean that they see the way to live the Christian life by observing our lives.

This is a problem, because in many homes the parents do not lead, they profess.

To lead is to live, not just profess.

To teach is not to give lessons, but to live the life.

Children have to go to Sunday School to learn that they should not fight. Why? Because mom and dad fight in the home. Daddy steals pencils from the office and brings them home to write with, so the children have to go to Sunday School to learn that they are not to steal.

Mom and dad become irritable and bad-tempered. Where are the children going to learn that they shouldn't be bad-tempered? In Sunday School! And this generates a further problem, because the teacher also may have a bad temper during the week...but not on Sunday!

So many of us are involved in a religious system. It is not real—it is playing games. The church meetings are not the most important part of our spiritual lives. It is the days in between—at the office and in the home—which are the most important part of our lives, not the two hours a week we are in the church building.

When the Lord sees you coming to the church service with your Bible under your arm, He says to the angels, *"We can go and have a rest. They are going to behave nicely here. So let's take a nap. But be ready for when they get out!"*

"Oh, hello Brother!" exclaims the pastor when you arrive.

"Bless you, Pastor," you answer, dressed in your Sunday best.

The pastor thinks to himself, "How spiritual these people are!" But who knows what happens at home?

Don't think that you fool God because you hold hands when you sit together in church. No, God knows more about you than that.

Even under the law, before the revelation of Jesus Christ, God said that they were to teach His ways to their children continually. It was to be a whole way of life from the time they got up to the time they went to bed. It was to be a process of continual teaching by example.

The home—not our religious organizations and church system—was meant to be the center of the Christian life. We need to gear the church to putting things back into their proper perspective.

Yes, the only complicated thing in the law was the sacrificial and temple system. And we don't need to do those things now. Jesus offered one all-sufficient sacrifice forever, abolishing all of the rituals. What God intended all along was a way of life, not a religion.

We come now to the New Testament. How did Jesus teach?

Do you see Him telling people, "Come to hear me Sunday mornings at ten o'clock?"

Can you imagine Him saying, "We are going to buy a piece of land in front of the central park in Jerusalem, so that our offices are in the best location, and we will have our church building next to our headquarters?"

We don't read of Him planning for a church of 60,000 members, larger than the Jewish church. He never said, "Let's hold a prayer meeting to see if we can find a piece of land on which to build our church."

Jesus' method of teaching was revolutionary from the outset.

When someone asked Him, "Master, where do you live?" He didn't say, "Here's a tract. You will find on the back that you can hear Me every Sunday morning at My church."

No, He just said, "Come and see."

And since He didn't have a permanent home, people had to follow Him for three years until He died. Those who were waiting for Him to set up a headquarters are still waiting, because He never had a fixed address.

He had no schedule of meetings—no Bible studies, prayer meetings, or Sunday morning services at which He would ring the bell and stand at the door saying, "Welcome, good morning. Are you well? Enjoy the meeting."

Jesus was a very simple, natural person who came to live among men, and by so doing to teach them how to live.

How did He teach?

Well, He taught when He got up. As He walked the roads of Palestine, He was teaching. When He sat down, people gathered around and He taught them. It was a way of life, 24 hours a day. He just lived, spontaneously. When He found one person, He lived with that person. When He found a thousand, He lived with a thousand.

"Follow Me!" said Jesus. "Learn of Me," He told them. "I *am*."

We say, "Don't look at me, look at the Bible. Follow the Bible."

We mean, "I tried and I couldn't do it. You see if you can do it."

Paul taught the same way as Jesus.

"You have become followers of me and of Christ," he told people. "Be imitators of me, as I am of Christ."

Most of our teaching today is so that people might come to know what we know, rather than that they come to be what we are. But to teach as Jesus and Paul taught is to share life, not just to share concepts. They communicated life in order that people would come to be like they were.

Paul said to the Corinthians, "You are the letters of Christ, read by all men."

We are God's letters! How sad that there needs to be a modern Bible called the *Living Bible*, when we are to be the living letters of Christ.

How are we to teach?

Our love, our joy, our peace should be read by every person, so that they will say, "What do you have that we don't?"

We have Him! He is the way, the truth, and the life. And when they see Him, they will want Him too.

Once a group of people asked me, "Do you believe in extra-biblical revelation?" I told them that we all believe in it, because where else could our church system have come from? It's not in the Bible—you won't find it there. So it must be an extra-biblical revelation if it is really from God.

Peter, Paul, James—none of them ever had the kind of system we have today. They taught wherever they were. They taught along the road. They taught any place and every place—on the beach, in the jails, at every opportunity.

They baptized people at four in the morning. It didn't matter what time it was. They never waited for the next church service. Any time was good enough; any place was fine. In a person's home; in the middle of the night, as in the case of the Philippian jailor; in the desert, as with the Ethiopian eunuch. It was a life, not a religious system.

Now I am not trying to say that we have to try to carry our religion over into the rest of the week. No, no, no! I am saying something much more radical than that. I believe that we need to abolish our religion!

To live in the Spirit is to be guided, not by a system of religion, but by the inner presence of God. It is a continual, built-in guidance system for the whole of life. And when we live this life, we become normal people.

Let me illustrate what I mean. In the beginning when God made Adam and Eve, their relationship with Him was very, very simple. I imagine that when God visited them in the garden, He said, "Adam, Eve! How are you?"

"Oh, good morning. We are fine. How are you?" they answered.

"Good. What are you doing, Adam?"

"Well, I am watering the strawberries."

"Are they coming nicely?"

"Beautiful, Father. You know, we gathered a basketful of them and Eve made jam."

"Is that so?"

"Yes, it was very tasty!"

This is how they communed with God. They fellowshipped with Him over the ordinary things of life. He was interested in everything they were doing.

God continued to inquire about their well-being. "Eve, how is everything?"

"Wonderful, Father. This garden is so nice. The temperature is perfect. Everything is so beautiful. It is really comfortable living here."

Many of us don't realize that it was this way. We associate God only with a system of religion, not with normal life. We think that when God called their names Adam said, "Quick, Eve, get on the organ, please. 'All hail the power of....'"

No, it was simpler than that. It was more natural.

Jesus brought to earth the kingdom of God so that it could spread throughout the whole world, transforming the whole of life.

He wanted people to be born into the kingdom so that they could live in the Spirit 24 hours a day, enjoying the kind of continual relationship God intended from the beginning. At last mankind would enter into fellowship with God in every aspect of life, just as He had planned when He created the human race.

9

Church Without Buildings?

What is the place of buildings in our church system?

We give lip-service to the concept of God's people as the church, but actually we speak of our buildings as the church most of the time. "I'm going to church," we say. But that is wrong.

It is old covenant. We continually are trying to push people from the old covenant into the new covenant, but we ourselves have a mixture of both covenants. It is as if we were in bed with one husband, then in bed with another; we are a bit with the law, and a bit with Jesus.

We have been seeing that whatever was spoken before Pentecost concerned, in the main, a God who was outside of people. He gave a law, and people had to study it and try to do it.

Since Pentecost, God is on the inside. He leads us from within. This is what it is to walk in the Spirit. And it is a very different thing from the old covenant.

Under the old covenant, they went to church. But in the new covenant, we are the church!

This is not just a concept, it is a reality. And if we don't understand it, we are going to be very mixed up. We are going to be engaging in spiritual adultery, trying to live with both Jesus and the law.

The old covenant put the meeting place in the center, and we have copied that system. But when we put the building in the center, we are all wrong because we are reverting to an old covenant situation—to a religious system.

Actually, we prefer a religious system in many cases because we can go to church on Sunday, then the rest of the week is ours. We do what we want then.

The commandment given to the apostles was, "Go into all the world."

But what do we say? "Let the sinners come to the church building."

Jesus never sang, "Come home, come home; ye who are weary, come home." He said, *"Go ye, go ye; ye who are lazy, go ye."*

He never said, *"How beautiful are the tongues of those who preach the Gospel."* No, He said, "the feet"—how beautiful are the feet of those who take the good news to every nation. It is a walking affair, a "going" thing. It is continual mobilization.

Our attitude is that we want a nice religion which makes us feel comfortable.

"Let's see how this pastor looks," we say to ourselves. "Ah, I don't like him. He's too short. He speaks too long. And I don't like the organ, either." This may be a common attitude, but it has nothing to do with the kingdom of God. Jesus didn't come to begin a nice club in which we all could feel comfortable.

Jesus never said, "Go into all the world and build temples and create church structures."

No, He said, "Destroy this temple, and I will build it up in three days." He was speaking of replacing the physical building with His own body. He was going to put a living temple in place of a stone temple. He was referring to you and me, who are His body, His temple. We have replaced the physical building.

The best years of the church, when the believers grew faster spiritually, had more power, more gifts, more revelation, and greater numerical expansion, came when they had no buildings.

We have so many other things in place of the Spirit. We have Bible commentaries, Sunday School materials, beautiful buildings, pianos and organs. The Spirit could leave many of our churches, and we wouldn't notice it. In fact, many churches don't even know whether they have the Spirit or not!

The effect of this is to divide our lives into two—the spiritual, and the secular.

When it comes to our home, our work, our time, we say, "Pastor, don't touch. This is my personal life, so keep your hands off. Don't I come to the meetings? Don't I pay tithes? What more do you want of me? I am a faithful member of your church."

We think that the Christian life is in our meetings. Everything that we do in the building is the Christian life.

When the "alleluia's" are over we say, "Hello, did you see what the inflation rate is up to? Who do you think is going to win the election?" This is our other life—our personal, secular life which we live until the next meeting.

"Oh, he's a fine Christian! He comes every Sunday, and he attends all of the meetings during the week. He doesn't smoke, and he doesn't drink. What more can I ask?" says the pastor.

I'm not against meetings and buildings, but I am saying that Christ is the center. Going to meetings, in itself, is nothing in God's eyes. That's just religion. Jesus came to bring us life, 24 hours a day. He came to bring a new, alternative society, the kingdom of God.

In the primitive church they lived one life. We have one life with its focal point in the church building: this is our spiritual life. A second is our secular or home life.

Some good people have gotten mixed up trying to maintain two centers.

As soon as we moved to our new house we started to witness to our neighbor.

"Yes, I am a Christian," the neighbor said.

"Oh, wonderful," said my wife. "Which church do you attend?"

"I don't attend a church. It is a long story, but I will tell you in a few words," she answered.

"I went to a church. And I liked it, really. The pastor preached so well. I went to the front and they took my name. I started to go on Sunday mornings. But then the pastor told me that if I really wanted to be in God's favor I should go on Sunday evenings also. So I started to go Sunday evenings.

"Then the pastor said I should go to the Bible study as well. So along I went to the Bible study. Then they said, 'Why don't you also come to Sunday School?' So after the church service I stayed for Sunday School.

"Next they said, 'You should come to the prayer meeting.' Well, I started going to the prayer meeting also. And then it was, 'But you must belong to the women's society.' So I had to go on Wednesdays to the women's society. Someone noticed that I had a good voice, so they said, 'You have to join the choir because you have a good voice. You must use your talents to the full for Jesus.' That meant I had to go to the choir practice on Thursdays.

"I was in church almost every day, and I was neglecting my house and family. One day I said, 'I won't go any more, except Sunday.'

"The pastor began making all sorts of indirect comments such as, 'Oh, those Sunday comers.' It seemed to me this was because I no longer went to all the meetings. After several more Sundays, I stopped going."

Of course some people like to go to meetings all the time. Often it is because they have emotional needs. They weep when the pastor preaches nicely, or during beautiful songs.

If you need an emotional release, you can see a motion picture that will cause you to weep. But the Lord put you into this world to save the world, to expand His kingdom, not to be entertained and to have your emotions touched in church meetings.

We are the light of the world. And the light has to be spread out to really light up the world. God put you in your neighborhood, and you are the light in that neighborhood. You are meant to shine there, in that darkness.

What does it mean to be a light? To be a light is to be a priest to all who are connected to the structure of your life.

First, I am to be the priest of my own home. The Bible clearly tells us this comes before anything else. If I am not a good priest there, there is little I can teach you.

The first requirement for those of us who are going to lead other people is that we are to have our own house in order—our own children in obedience to us at home.

When you read the requirements of a minister in Paul's first letter to Timothy, it doesn't say it is essential to believe in the millennium, in the Trinity, or in the tribulation. It says a minister has to be the husband of one wife, a respectable person; and he has to have his house in order. He also has to be hospitable. His family life is to be open for all to see.

In my situation, I travel a great deal—sometimes more than 50 percent of the time.

The Bible says a husband and wife can separate for a period of time if they are in common agreement. So when I travel, it has to be in full agreement. If my wife would not agree, I would have trouble. My life is committed to Martha and my children, so they come first.

When I was a pastor and also traveling, I saw it was too much. We decided I would have to give up pastoring, or give up traveling, because both things were too much for the family. So I gave up pastoring.

I was living in Buenos Aires and traveling around the world. I had to fly many hours to each place. The tickets were very expensive, so that meant I had to be away a month on each trip, and sometimes two months, which was bad.

We looked at how we could improve the situation. We decided to move to a more central location, close to an airport, here in the United States.

But there was still room for improvement.

One day my wife said, "When you come back from your trips, you have to go to the office and answer all the mail and plan your next schedule. I propose to help, so that when you come home you can be with the family more. I will answer all your mail."

Now, every evening I call Martha, no matter where I am.

We talk about all the things that she is thinking about. We discuss the mail and decide how we should answer it. Even the letters which arrive while I am at home, I leave and she answers them when I am gone.

I also do all my studying and reading on airplanes and in hotels. And I write all my cards and letters then. I do nothing at home. So at home I just have fun with my family.

We get up together, we do the beds together, we do the shopping together. And I cook when I am at home to give my wife a break from the kitchen. We do the gardening together, we paint...we do everything as a family. The children are included when they are at home. We go to soccer games, to concerts—wherever my family goes, I go with them.

We have adjusted to my traveling. This is Christ in us, showing us how to be creative in our situation. We have learned how to live in the situation with joy, not just bearing it, suffering it, or merely accepting it.

So Martha stays at home with joy, and I travel with joy; and we are very happy.

The idea came to me of having family meetings, like a business meeting. We have them every few months. We start with a special dinner, for which we all dress up in our best clothes. Then, after dinner we take our coffee into the living room, and we have a meeting in which everyone can say whatever he feels.

Our children tell us what they think we are doing wrong. And many times they have been right.

Before, instead of really listening to them we just rebuked them or punished them. But now, we listen to them as they explain their points of view. And even if they are wrong, we often see that they have the right motivation—and we should judge the motives, not merely the actions. So we listen to them, and they listen to us; and after we have talked everything out fully we make decisions.

We have made adjustments in our home in order to allow me to continue my teaching ministry. Actually, the reason I travel is because of our church system. I would not need to do it if the church were structured differently. But it is necessary because of the system. So we have made changes in our home to allow for it, because if I didn't direct my home properly I could not go and preach to others.

To be a light, the first place I must shine is in the home. This is my first responsibility.

10

Let's Tell God
So He Can Be Glad

If our families were as loving and harmonious as God intends them to be, we would be a powerful witness in our communities.

If we are not effective priests at home, we cannot be good priests anywhere. So I want to share some of the things I have learned in my own family. These are not just concepts, they are life. I experience what I am talking about.

As a pastor, I gave good instruction about the family. But there is a big difference between teaching a concept and imparting life. A man may have a family altar, so that his family starts the day with perfect teaching. He tells others to try to do what he teaches. But when you try to do it, you wonder if he does what he says!

To have even perfect teaching, but not to actually do it, is legalism—a concept. And that condemns people. Although you may not live it, you can look in the Bible and pick out verses to give a wonderful picture of marriage. But if you are not experiencing what you are teaching, people who hear you will find they can't do it, and become condemned.

One of the greatest blessings for the leaders of my church was to come and stay in our home when I was a pastor. I invited them to be with us for two or three days, to see how we lived.

They said, "You know, Brother Ortiz, the greatest help to

us is to see that you are normal people. We thought you and your wife spoke with Bible verses, and that you got up in the morning singing hymns.''

Remember, the Pharisee looked like a saint, but he was a holy hypocrite. The publican, on the other hand, was an honest sinner. And I prefer an honest sinner to a holy hypocrite.

So I believe that we have to start by being very honest. We have to take off our masks, and let people see us as we really are. We cannot be one way in our church fellowships and a different way at home. We should be the same all the time.

What is worse, we not only live a different life on Sunday morning from the rest of the week, many of us live two lives in our own homes. We have family devotions at which we behave in a saintly way, different from the rest of the day.

If I said that we don't have family devotions, I would not be telling the truth. But if I say we do have them, you will think that we have them in the traditional way—a family altar. And that is not altogether correct.

I believe that one of the greatest inheritances we can give our children is that we are not activity-oriented Christians. By that I mean that Christ is not something for Tuesdays, Thursdays at 7:30 p.m. and Sundays at 10:00 a.m., or from 6:00 to 6:30 in the mornings. No, Christ is 24 hours a day. We are in a continual dialogue with that inner Christ. It is continual fellowship because we have become one.

So when my children and I are playing soccer, or while we are doing anything together, we stop in the break and we say, ''How nice is this day. We're having fun, aren't we?''

They tell me that they are having great fun. So I say, ''Let's tell God, so He can be glad.''

Then I say, ''Lord, we are having fun, thanks to You.''

We don't close our eyes and make it a religious act. In fact, there isn't one instance of anyone closing his eyes to pray anywhere in the Bible (although of course it's all right to do so if we want to). We just talk with God naturally, and we recognize Him in everything. So my children have learned to have a relationship and not a religion.

When we get up in the morning we say, "Good morning! Wake up! Look what a beautiful day it is. Isn't God good!"

Then at the breakfast table—sometimes we pray before eating, and sometimes we don't. Sometimes I say just a word, without making it like a prayer, such as, "Thank you, Lord."

Other times I tell my children how good God is to give us all this food. It's not a prayer, yet it is a prayer. I try not to make them religious, but to live this life in Christ in a perfectly natural way.

We try to treat our children in the way that God treats us. This means that we deal with them through relationship rather than through law. I believe this is the key: relationship and friendship. Not their perfection, but dialogue.

When I get home after a trip, all of our children come to our bedroom at night.

We are six—my wife and I, and four of them. We all lie in the bed talking, sometimes for three or four hours. Every night that happens when I am home. When they have to go to school, we have to push them out. But when they don't have school, I tell my wife, "Let them stay. Even if we fall asleep, let them talk among themselves and with us about everything."

My wife tells me that even when I am away they come to our room. The older ones work in a restaurant. So sometimes they have to close the restaurant at 12:00 or 1:00. Even when they come home at 1:00 in the morning, they come to our room. They wake us up, and we talk with them.

My children are all teenagers now, and we have to understand that teenagers are teenagers. When they grow up, they will be grown-ups; but right now they are teenagers, so we face many of the situations that other parents face.

The first thing that my wife and I see is that we are not to worry. Teenage is a normal stage of growth—we all have been teenagers, too. We believe our example is sufficient to see them through these years, so we don't try to hurry it or worry about it.

We don't get shocked or scandalized when they do something which is "wrong" according to our evangelical rules. Like kissing a girl, or smoking a cigarette.

We have developed such an atmosphere in our home that they tell us when they do something like kiss a girl. We are very, very good friends. So we know what they do. We know where they go. They tell us things I never would have told my parents when I was their age!

I believe that the most important thing is not to require perfection from them, but to accept them as teenagers and require from them honesty. As they grow, they will learn what is expedient for them, and what is not expedient.

Honesty is the key thing. We talk with them in such a way that they don't live under condemnation. We don't say, "God will punish you," or "You are going to lose your soul."

If your children can tell you everything they do, don't worry if sometimes they tell you something that might be bad. Because they will do it anyway, but not tell you. So you are better to know, then you have an opportunity to teach them gradually. The other way, you are going to lose them.

I find that this is the way God is with us. He wants us to trust and love Him. So even if we do something wrong, we do it in His presence because He lives in us. We are friends, and a friend understands. When we explain, He hears us and forgives us, and we keep our friendship.

Most Christians are related to a set of rules rather than to a person. The set of rules has no emotions, no feelings—you cannot talk to them. It's just, "Thou shalt not."

But we are related to a a personal God who has feelings and emotions. He listens, understands, and dialogues with us— and we can tell Him as did Peter.

"Lord, You ask me if I love You, and I say yes," Peter said. *"But You ask me again and again. Listen, I know You saw*

my denying You. I denied You three times. But though I denied You, I love You. You may say, 'How do you love Me if you deny Me?' Anyway, Lord, I don't understand; but I know that I love You. If You know everything, You know I love You, in spite of all I did."

My children, though they are just like other children, have a relationship with Jesus. He loves them, and they love Him. They are not saints. Though they are not perfect by all outer appearances, they have a relationship with Him.

The power of sin is the law. Therefore, children will be more tempted to things which are prohibited to them than to things which are not prohibited.

This means they are free to decide not to do certain things, because they see that they are not expedient for them. As Paul says, "All things are lawful for me, but not all things are profitable."

They are free to tell us about anything they do.

If they do something wrong, they know that we will react with full acceptance. We would never reject them. Also we will always be there to help them out in any situation, rather than to reprove, threaten or condemn. They have to see the love of the Father in us. Some issues are not easy, but I believe the way to deal with them is to do so openly, rather than avoiding them.

We were concerned that our children might marry too early. But David said, "No, no, Daddy. I am going to marry when I'm 26, like you."

I believe they have a very high idea of marriage and the home, because since they were tiny children they have seen us living the life of Christ with them openly.

Because we are in Christ, we have no problems, just new situations. So I am never anxious for anything. I rest. I face each situation at the time and follow the inner guidance of the Spirit. There are no formulas, just the daily leading of the inner Christ.

Acceptance is always the underlying basis for all we do in our relationship with our children. Acceptance is through the blood of Jesus, not by their behavior. Up to now, what our children have seen in us is what they believe will be good for them also.

Of course, it is not so easy if parents have come to a knowledge of the Lord when their children already are 15 or 16, and they already are rebellious.

In such a situation I would tell my children, "I want you to know that whatever you do, I love you. But I want to explain what I believe about the situation you are in. You are wrong. Whether you obey me or not will not change my love for you. But because I love you, I have to tell you when you are wrong."

I would tell them everything they need to hear, because love isn't keeping quiet. But I would stress that it doesn't matter what they do, I will love them anyway.

"Do the wrong," I would tell them, "and I'm still your friend. But I have to advise you that you are wrong."

We will have more success this way, I believe, than if we put their obedience to us as a requirement for our friendship. If we continue to be their friends, they will face us every day and there may be a chance to help them.

But if we tell them, "If you don't do what I say, goodbye," they are on their own and we no longer can influence them. While they are in our home, we are a convicting factor. And as we continue to love them, one day they will listen.

First of all, then, our children need to know that they are fully accepted by us just as they are.

They must know that they don't have to perform in order to earn love and acceptance. This is very important, because our children learn of God through us. The picture they have of us, their parents, is the picture they probably will have of God. So we have to be careful to treat them as God treats us—and the way that God accepts us and dwells in us is just as we are.

Once one of our children did something quite bad. He was six or seven, so we sent him to bed. When I passed by the bedroom he called me and using a Spanish expression, said, "I'm so tranquil." I asked him why he was tranquil. "Because I know that though you spank me, you love me."

Even in that little mind, that was the concept he had of God. My children never thought they would be rejected by God because I taught them that they are always accepted.

Second, I also believe that discipline is necessary.

Discipline is not legalism, however. Legalism is when they have to perform to be accepted. Discipline is with acceptance. They know that whatever they do, they will be accepted. But they have to learn what is expedient for them.

Discipline is just part of the infrastructure of the house. "Brush your teeth," "Say please" and "Sit properly" are part of the running of the house.

Third, I also have learned that spanking and shouting at my children don't do too much toward the end we are pursuing. When they do not understand other language, perhaps a spanking could be good, especially when they are quite small. But they have to understand very well why the spanking is given, and that we love them.

My concern is that when many parents spank their children, it's not to the degree of the child's obedience but rather as a result of the parents' impatience. When we are in a good mood, we often are too lenient. This confuses children.

Fourth, look for guidance from the Lord. I don't have a rigid concept of how to discipline. Instead, I believe I am led spontaneously by the Lord.

Every child is different. Sometimes a child will understand much more by a spanking than by words; at other times, a spanking would be a very wrong thing to give him. Those of us who live in the Spirit learn how to be led by the Lord in the way we approach our children when they do wrong.

Do you understand what I mean when I say that the life of

the Spirit is not for services on Sundays, but for the whole of life? I need the guidance of the Holy Spirit in my home with the children more than in meetings!

Sometimes people think that the Holy Spirit is only for devotional times, and they deal with their family affairs by books or rules. No, it is in all things that we are to follow the guidance of Jesus in us.

If we would follow the Spirit, our homes would be a witness in the community. But too often our homes are a mess. Our homes must come ahead of any ministry that we are involved in.

One time we faced a difficult situation in our family, and I was ready to quit the ministry.

I called a family meeting and told my children, "Perhaps I am the guilty one, because I travel so much that I cannot be here at home. Mom is a woman, and you take advantage of her. So I will have to stop traveling. I will take a job, and I will make disciples around where I live, because you are of more importance than my ministry."

My two sons said, "Listen, Daddy. We are sure that your ministry is from God. We have seen the blessings that have come to people around the world because of it. People tell us continually, 'Your daddy helped me in this or that.' We will do our part, so you can stay in the ministry. We are going to behave better. We are going to obey Mom. We are not going to take advantage of her."

So we made a unanimous decision that I would keep traveling.

What does the neighbor know about the Christian in many situations? Only that in this house a Christian lives. He's a very strange person. He leaves early in the morning and comes back late at night. That's all the neighbor knows. He has no fellowship, no contact with this mysterious man.

It should not be this way. So the first thing we have to do is become a family that is a light in the community, that spreads love to all who live around us. And this begins when our family is in submission to Christ, the head of the home.

11

What About Your Relatives?

When my parents came to the Lord, in no time at all we started to fellowship with those in the church which we had begun attending. They became our whole interest.

Do you know what our relatives said? "Since they got into that religion, we lost them."

It was the truth. We were so busy with the church that we lost all contact with our friends, relatives and former acquaintances. We saw our relatives only at funerals. The very ones we were meant to bring to the Lord were suddenly no longer a part of our lives.

Who are the ones who bring new people to the Lord?

Those who have themselves just been converted, because they still have friends in the world. But after a few months they won't bring any more new people because they will cut themselves off from all their friends. They will burn their bridges with the world and, instead, will come to prayer meetings and Bible studies, becoming totally absorbed in the church system.

I recall the time when our family belonged to an Italian church. We had meetings every evening except Friday. Six evenings out of the week we were away from our home!

Each evening at 6:30 we left home with our Bibles under our arms. We had no car at that time, so we had to walk seven blocks to take the train. We didn't return until around

10:30 p.m.

Imagine what our neighbors thought! Every day at 6:30 they watched us leave. They were sorry for us. "Poor people. What a religion they have!"

Of course, we had no time to make friends with them—we were so busy with the church. Even when there was a holiday, the church held a special meeting. We were always in church, so there was no room for our relatives or our neighbors in our lives. We thought that spirituality was to be in church continually.

God saved each of us to spread His kingdom in the place in which He put us, in the structure of life in which we find ourselves. We are responsible for the people who are around us. He wants us to reach them, to show them His love. He desires to love them through us. This is how the kingdom of God grows.

But the church has too often extracted us from the normal structures of the world. We have cut all connections with the people we were meant to spread light to. The result is that we are useless for evangelism.

We need to look afresh at the purpose for the church. It was never meant to be an institution separate from life. To become a Christian was meant to be the normal way to live.

When God called Abraham, do you know what He had in mind? "In you shall all the families of the earth be blessed," He told him. But what did the Jews do? They thought God's blessing was just for them; they wanted the privilege, but not the responsibility.

God has not put us in His church to be lazy. He expects a great deal of us.

We are the true seed of Abraham through Christ. God intends that through us all nations come into the blessing of Abraham. We are here to extend the kingdom of God into the whole world.

God spreads us out all over the place so that we can salt the earth and light the world. Everyone is meant to shine in the place that God has placed him. This is how the kingdom of God invades the structures of society, like leaven spreading through the whole loaf of bread.

Jesus said, "Seek first the kingdom." So the first thing in our lives is the kingdom. Every single one of us is in the place that God means him to be for the extension of the kingdom.

This means that it is very important when we move that we ask God where He wants us. We should not just move for ourselves, but because God wants us as one of His representatives in a new location.

"Well, I changed my job because...," we say.

But that is wrong. We change jobs because God is taking us from one job to another, because He needs a missionary in our new work situation.

If you are studying at a university, you aren't there primarily to get a degree. You are there first and foremost for the kingdom. Obtaining the degree is part of your work in the kingdom, not simply so that you can fatten your intellect.

A boy came from Peru to study at the university in our country. After a while, he got saved. He came to our Assembly church. A few weeks later he told the pastor, "I don't want to study any more."

"Why?" asked the pastor.

"Because now I'm saved," he replied.

"What do you mean?" the pastor inquired. "You can't leave your studies because you are saved!"

"No, I was not really studying there."

"But we saw you studying there."

"Yes, I had to study; but I was not there for that purpose. The Communist party of Peru sent me to the Argentine university to spread Communism in the university. In order to do that, I had to become a regular student. My studies were a cover-up. When I had finished this degree, I would study for another, and another, staying as long as I could to spread

Communism."

If you are in a university, you are there first to spread God's kingdom. If you can't preach, you can shine as a light. You can love people, so that they see that Christ is alive today.

Suppose you work at Ford Motor Company. "Well, I'm there because they pay better, and because they have so many benefits," you tell me.

No, you are at Ford Motor Company because God needed a missionary there.

He simply uses Mr. Ford to support you in the mission field.

If you have two lives—a private life, and a religious life—you can work in a place for many personal reasons. But when you live only one life, God is in everything you do. And wherever you find yourself, you are responsible to those who are a part of the structure of your life.

First, we are responsible to our own family. The pastor isn't responsible; he is just a helper, a counselor. We are the responsible ones. Husbands are responsible to their wives and children.

"But I am a widow." Then you are responsible. If there is no husband, you are the priest.

"We are orphans, and I am the only one who is saved." Then you are responsible to your brothers and sisters.

Whatever household you live in, you are responsible. God appointed you to that household to be the head.

By "head," I do not mean the person giving orders. I am talking about being the spiritual light in the household, the priest. If you live in a students' residence and you are the only saved person, you are responsible to those students who live with you in that household, whether you like it or not.

In every household where there is someone who knows the Lord, he is responsible. He is the light to that house, the priest. And God will ask each of us, "What did you do in the place in which I put you?"

Second, after our immediate family we are responsible to

our relatives—our uncles, aunts and cousins.

"But it is 20 years since I last saw them!" Yes, and that is very wrong; because you are responsible to them.

Third, you are responsible to your friends. Not just your close friends, but also your lawyer and your dentist. If God has saved you, it is because He wants to reach through you all of these people who are a part of the structure of your life. If not through you, then through whom?

Fourth, you are responsible to your neighbors. You are the priest in your neighborhood.

"Me?"

Yes, you are the pastor of that neighborhood. The church divides the world into provinces, the provinces into dioceses, the dioceses into parishes, and the parishes into homes. Every Christian has a parish.

Your block is your parish. You are responsible to that block. Do you imagine God is going to send an angel from heaven to evangelize your block so that you can go to meetings?

You are the pastor of your little parish, and the minister is your counselor. He is there to help give you confidence and to assist you in fulfilling your responsibility by providing guidance. But you are the responsible one.

You are also responsible to your fellow workers. You are a priest to those who work around you each day. They are a part of the structure which God wants His light to permeate through you.

So this means that you have something to do. Perhaps you should start by making a list of all the people you are responsible to.

But before you begin, I want to draw a very clear distinction between the concept and life.

If you have just the concept of being responsible as a priest in your parish, you will either find it a tremendous burden, or you will rush out and try to convert everyone by preaching to him. The letter kills. If your responsibility is just a concept to you, it will either kill you—or you will kill those to whom you witness because you will turn them off!

I am not speaking about trying to do some great work for Jesus. I am talking about a life which so manifests love that it attracts people to the light. In other words, our life lived 24 hours a day in Him is itself doing the work of the kingdom of God.

When I am invited to speak in churches, I am afraid of one thing. Most of the invitations are to speak on discipleship, which is a subject I really like to speak about. But the danger is that we become more attached to the method than to the living Jesus Christ.

Humans find the mechanical part of discipleship very tempting. It is attractive to us. We get hold of the concept, but not the life; and it ends up becoming another system, another form of bondage.

In the situation in which discipleship arose, in the church fellowship which I pastored in Argentina, it did not come to us in a mechanical way at all. It came as life.

We did not know anything about discipleship. We were simply living as a fellowship and discovering things without knowing what we were really doing. Only after I came to the United States and started to teach was it labeled discipleship.

People said to me, "You are teaching the doctrine of submission."

For the first time we discovered that we were practicing discipleship! Until that time it had just been a flow of life, not a doctrine. When we discovered the doctrine of submission, we spoiled the life! So I am afraid of the label.

When I am invited to speak on discipleship, I now prefer not to speak on that subject the first visit. Rather, on the first visit, I prepare people for what is to come. Through my first visit they understand that I am not legalistic in any sense at all. Only when they understand this will I speak on discipleship.

You remember that when Paul visited Athens, he found that the Athenians liked to spend their time hearing new doctrines.

Sometimes I think that we are like that in our churches. We all like to hear what Brother Cho did in Korea, or what God did in our church in Argentina.

Those things are interesting. And they can be helpful. But we really don't need to copy them because we all have the same Spirit living within us to lead us in our particular church situations. The danger is that we take these things and create a new system out of them. They become a formula.

In this book, I am not trying to present you with a new system. I am simply seeking to present to you the living Jesus Christ who can tell you what to do in your local situation. This is not a new recipe on how the church should be. It is to point you to the Holy Spirit who can lead you 24 hours a day.

My purpose in talking about how we made disciples and how the kingdom grew in our situation is to make you think. I want to cause you to look again at the preconceived concepts you have of how the church should be and how to win disciples. You need to be free to hear what the Holy Spirit is saying.

I would like to be a disturbing element. Before we can be open to hear what the Spirit is saying to our churches, we need to be brainwashed from our lifeless forms. We need to abandon our fixed concepts of the church so that we can experience the ever-fresh life of Jesus on a continual basis.

When I speak of being a light in our communities, and of being priests to those who are a part of the structure of our lives, you have a picture of what I mean. But I don't mean what you picture. Those concepts are not part of the life of Christ. They are part of our church system.

I am not talking about trying to get your relatives, workmates, friends and neighbors to come to church. Nor am I speaking of giving them tracts with Bible verses to convince them that they need Christ. That is all part of our system. Most of them are not interested in those things, because they are religion and not life.

I don't know how to say this...I don't think there is an easy way to say it. I think I just have to say it, even if it seems hard.

I believe there is coming a time of great shaking of all of our systems, and only that which is unshakeable because it is the life of Christ will not be torn down.

Times are coming when we are not going to have pipe organs, and when we may not have hymn books and Sunday School materials.

We even may be without Bibles! But the primitive church didn't have any of these things. The New Testament hadn't been written yet. And most believers didn't have access to the Old Testament. All they had was the Holy Spirit. But because they had Him 24 hours a day, they had the kind of faith that cannot be shaken.

As a result, they turned the world upside down!

You see, a church system may become a hindrance. It ought to be something that helps us bring people to Christ, but instead it ends up being a problem. We have added so many things that we are caught up in, and we don't know how to get rid of them. We even think that they are essential.

Let me illustrate what I mean by a hindrance. Our church in Argentina is charismatic. We raise our hands when we sing. (Well, sometimes we do and sometimes we don't.)

Now that doesn't appeal to everybody, so the system has become a hindrance for many people. Once we invited a certain family to our church.

"No, I don't think we want to come. We don't fit into your atmosphere," they said.

Some people feel better in a Baptist atmosphere, or in a Catholic atmosphere, or in an Episcopal atmosphere. I'm not justifying the attitude, but I do wonder if sometimes the things we do in our churches aren't a major reason why the world doesn't want to come to them. Most of these things are just not normal: they are religious.

You know, most of the people you are responsible to will

not come if you invite them to church. But did you ever think of inviting them to your house? They will come there.

If you bring a person to a Pentecostal church, or a Baptist or Episcopal church, he has to overcome many things in order to get to Christ.

Perhaps he is anti-catholic, anti-charismatic, or anti-liturgy...But he is not anti-ice cream!

So you bring him to your house. Your home, not the church building, now becomes the center of your Christian activities. When the church is centered in a home, it is more likely to be centered in people than in a building.

The key is that every home starts to function fully as a center. Every home, and every individual.

I am not talking about taking your car out of the garage and driving to someone else's home for a church meeting. No, that is just like going to a church building. I am speaking of bringing to your home all who are a part of your structure of life—your relatives, friends, neighbors and fellow workers.

Now I don't mean holding meetings in your home with gospel songs and Bible study. Some churches do that. They have a hundred members, so they divide them into four homes. But that is just another church of the kind that we have in buildings.

I am talking about staying in your house to fulfill your duties of priesthood. You begin with your wife. I was the pastor of the First Assembly of God, but my wife was neglected. Start by evangelizing your wife.

What do I mean by evangelizing?

To evangelize is to have complete love. It is to have fellowship, communion, full understanding between each other.

So evangelize your wife. Love her and meet her needs as the Holy Spirit prompts you. Then check your relationship with your children. How are you getting along with them?

What about your relatives?

How are you doing with your cousins and aunts? How long is it since you last saw them? Start to rebuild those burned bridges. I did it, and it is amazing how many we won to the Lord without speaking a word.

I wrote them, making friends with them again. I didn't preach. I shared love with them. I repented of neglecting them, rejecting them, because I had let the church system take all of my time. I won them just by loving them.

Those women whose husbands don't know the Lord—how many of them go to all the church meetings? No wonder their husbands don't come to the Lord. The church is their rival! They need to evangelize at home by showing the love of Christ as the Holy Spirit leads. He will tell you how to love if you listen to Him and do what He tells you to do.

An incident occurred in our church in Argentina which touched me deeply.

We brought a very nice family to the Lord. They were a wealthy family. He had been an atheist. But because of the healing of their daughter, the whole family was saved, and they became fully committed to the Lord.

This man started bringing people to his home. Eventually he had 30 of his friends and relatives meeting there. It took about a year and a half for this group to grow to that size, but when it reached that number the multiplication stopped.

After they had finished witnessing to all their friends, they couldn't win anyone else to the Lord. It's like when you start to sell encyclopedias in your spare time. After you sell them to your friends, you don't sell any more.

The same thing was happening with many other families. My wife said, "Johnny, those who are going to come to the Lord have already come; and those who haven't won't come."

There seemed to be a limit to growth, and we couldn't break through this limit. We decided to ask the Lord how we could keep on multiplying.

We asked this former atheist and his family, "Wouldn't many more of your friends and relatives come to the Lord if it didn't involve being linked with a church system?"

He thought about this, and the next day he told me, "Pastor, I am sure that many more would come, but our church system is the problem. It is a hindrance."

This started us studying.

If the church system is essential for salvation, let's push people into that system. But if the pipe organ, the hymns, the choir, the church calendar, the board, the deacons and Sunday School materials are not essential, then maybe we should ask the Lord if there is another way.

So we began to pray. And as the Lord directed us, we made radical changes. I am not suggesting that everybody should do this today, but it came as life to us. It was not a concept or a doctrine; we weren't trying to create a new kind of system.

This brother and his family had a large apartment. Instead of trying to bring more people to church, we encouraged him to make his own disciples at home. So he invited them to his apartment, not to a church service.

Six months later I visited him. He now had a church in his home of over 200 people! Some 250 of his relatives had been saved, and they were all filled with the Holy Spirit and fully committed to the Lord. But not one of them was coming to the church services.

Before we can win people to the Lord, we have to build relationships. Often they have been broken, so they must be repaired. Where there is a birthday, I give a little gift. Or perhaps I give a plant to my neighbor and start to build a friendship. I take every opportunity to win people as friends. Then the gospel will be passed on quite spontaneously through relationships.

Perhaps by now you imagine that I am against church buildings and all that goes with them. No, I am not against them. I believe that if we were to change the center of our activities from buildings to people in their homes, we would find a new use for the buildings.

If I could, I would add a few things to the buildings, actually.

I would add a swimming pool, a racquet ball court, and perhaps a sauna. Not everyone in the community can have a swimming pool or sauna at home, so there is a place for these in the community center of the church. The existing church buildings could be used for conferences when needed, as well as for special times of praise.

If we would get rid of the bondage of the building, we would begin to increase numerically. For the sake of the people, perhaps we need to close the building some Sundays. We don't need to hear a new message every Sunday. Once a month is quite adequate; then we have a month to put it into practice.

So the other Sundays, we can do the Lord's work. Instead of having a service next Sunday, everyone could invite some friend or relative to his home. Not to a religious meeting, but to build a relationship.

Take a church body which consists of 800 members, representing 200 or 300 homes. That means all of those families are evangelizing. When we use the church building, only the wife comes in many cases. But when we use the home, the husband, wife and children can all be together. So each Sunday 200 or 300 people are evangelized.

We would not be closing the church building down for three weeks out of four so that the people could stay home watching television, but so they could be involved in furthering the kingdom of God. They would open their homes—not to have advertized meetings—but to love their cousins, their aunts, their neighbors, their friends and those they work with.

After a month, when we returned to the building, it would not be large enough because of all the additional people who would have been won to the Lord through the month of evangelism. So the pastor would have to say, "The north side of the city will come in the morning, and the south side will come in the evening."

The following three weeks would be spent in the same kind of activity, so that after the second month the pastor would have to say, "The north side will come in the morning, the south side in the evening, and the southwest on Saturday evening."

Eventually, the building would be packed every day with different people from different areas of the city.

This was the way the primitive church functioned. You can see it in the New Testament. Every day, both in public places and in every home, they didn't cease the work of the Lord. We are forever talking about *starting* work for the Lord, but they *never ceased.*

We are a royal priesthood, to show forth the love of God to the world. We are ambassadors for Christ, sent to bring good news to all nations. It is time we make our church buildings serve us, instead of us serving them. When the church is centered in the person of Jesus Christ instead of in a religious system, the kingdom of God will spread throughout the whole earth as Jesus commanded.

12

Does God Have Any Needs?

Many people have a sneaking suspicion that God is mad at them.

Some believers feel deep down inside them that God is out to get them. Others think that He is only for those who are Christians.

But God is for everybody. He is the God of all nations, and He is for all people.

God is not the God of the Jews only, or of the Christians only. He loves the Arabs as much as He loves the Jews. He loves the North Americans, the Africans, and the South Americans. He loves them, and He is for them all.

How can we know that God loves us and is for us? He demonstrated this supremely, of course, in His Son. Jesus is the love of God in the form of a human being.

But Jesus Himself is no longer on the earth as a human being. So He has chosen those who believe in Him to show His love to the world. Believers are His representatives today. We are Christ to this world.

If people do not see the love of God in us, they will not see it at all. We are Christ's only means of expressing Himself in our three-dimensional realm. Either they see God's love through Christ dwelling in us, or they don't see it at all.

Centuries before Jesus came on earth, God selected a particular nation to show His love to the world.

That nation was Israel. He made a covenant, an agreement, with them. "Now then, if you will indeed obey My voice and keep my covenant, then you shall be My own possession among all the peoples, for all the earth is mine; and you shall be to Me a kingdom of priests and a holy nation" (Exodus 19:5-6).

When God called Israel, He called them with the world in mind. He is the God of all nations, and He called Israel to be a kingdom of priests to those nations. It was His intention to use them to show His love to mankind. He had in mind the whole creation, because of His promise to Adam and Eve concerning the serpent and the Redeemer who would come to deliver man. This Redeemer wasn't coming only to the Jewish people; He was coming to all nations, white, black, brown and yellow.

Why did God choose Israel?

He chose them because they were Abraham's descendants, and He had promised that through Abraham He would bless "all the families of the earth." Israelites were going to be the priests of God, to show His love to all the world.

But Israel became self-righteous.

"We are the people of God," they said. 'We are the chosen ones. Those other nations are the heathen. Pooh! We are the privileged ones, the holy nation."

They forgot the rest of the world. Not only did they not become priests for the rest of the nations, they came to the point where they needed priests themselves. They were chosen to be priests between God and the other nations, but they forgot their role to such an extent that God had to give them their own priest. So the Levites were chosen to confess the sins of the people and to offer sacrifices for them.

What about the rest of the world? The Jews' attitude was, let them die! To the Jews, other nations were garbage. So the job never got done. They didn't manifest God's love to the whole world.

Now the same words which were spoken to the people of

Israel at Mt. Sinai have been said to us who believe in Jesus.

"You also, as living stones, are being built up as a spiritual house for a holy priesthood, to offer up spiritual sacrifices acceptable to God through Jesus Christ...But you are a chosen race, a royal priesthood, a holy nation, a people for God's own possession, that you may proclaim the excellencies of Him who has called you out of darkness into His marvelous light" (I Peter 2:5,9).

In Acts 13 we see such priests in operation.

In the church at Antioch, there were prophets and teachers. Among them were Paul and Barnabas. They were "ministering to the Lord." They were functioning as priests. What were they saying? The Bible doesn't tell us. But to minister is to meet the needs of a person, and they were meeting the needs of God.

How did they minister to God?

For many years I never knew, because in seminary they taught us how to minister to people but never how to minister to God. But we can tell by the context what they were doing. The Spirit said, "Set apart for Me Barnabas and Saul for the work to which I have called them." Then the church "sent them away."

In other words, they had been asking the Lord, "What about the rest of the world, Lord?"

I admire the spirit of the Lord's people in Antioch. They never complained when the Lord took their pastors and sent them to the other nations. They didn't say, "No, we want that pastor to stay here. We are going to vote to keep him."

So, they were ministering by saying, *"Come on, Lord. What about the rest of the world?"*

God's answer was for them to separate the best pastors they had and send them out. Two of them, sent on their way by the Holy Spirit, went down to Selucia and from there to Cyprus. This was their first missionary trip. They were functioning as priests, a holy people, a chosen race.

What does the word priest mean?

It brings into our minds a man with long, black robes. But that is not it. A priest is a person who is between man and God. Another word is intercessor. It means one who stands between two parties. He wants to further God's kingdom—to promote God's business, God's ways, God's desires among men. He is also one who is concerned for man's business in the presence of God. He is an arbitrator between two parties, which is not a very easy job.

So really a priest is a friend.

He is a friend of God and has influence with God. He is also a friend of man and has influence with man. He ministers to man in favor of God, and ministers to God in favor of man

Sometimes it is not easy to be a friend of man and a friend of God at the same time. It is like being in the middle of a two-way road—you can be hit from both sides. But that is the whole essence of priesthood—to be a friend of both parties. If you do not have access, acceptance and friendship with both sides, you cannot be a priest.

What does it mean to function as a priest, as a minister, as an intercessor?

A minister is one who meets the needs of men. When a person is in need of hope, in need of healing, in need of forgiveness or in need of counseling, then the Lord uses different ones of His priests to meet those needs. So if I am given $1,000 to give to ten needy persons, it is my responsibility to administrate it for those ten people. And I think about how I am going to meet their needs in the most effective way.

But we also have to minister to God. "Does God have any needs?" you ask.

Believe it or not, God has tremendous needs. He is in great need of our service. This is why He appoints priests or intercessors.

Let me cite an instance from Scripture. You will find it in

Ezekiel 22. The whole chapter describes the horrible social, political and spiritual condition that the people of Israel were in.

It is summarized in verse 29: "The people of the land have practiced oppression and committed robbery, and they have wronged the poor and needy and have oppressed the sojourner without justice."

What was God's attitude toward this tragic state of affairs? "And I searched for a man among them who should build up the wall and stand in the gap before Me for the land, that I should not destroy it; but I found no one" (verse 30). Because He found no one, He had to punish them as a nation and deliver them to an enemy in order to put a stop to all of the suffering that they were bringing upon themselves.

God was upset by the way they were vexing the poor, the elderly and the defenseless. But God didn't want to destroy them for their sin. He was searching for just one person who would stand in the gap before Him on behalf of the nation of Israel, but He couldn't find one. If He had found one person with a heart like that, God would not have punished them. But there wasn't one priest, one intercessor, in the whole nation.

One of the greatest problems in the church today is that we do not believe in a personal, living God—an existentialist God. Instead, He is a set of rules and a set of doctrines. If we do what the rules say, and agree with the doctrines, we can feel safe. If we don't, we are fearful.

Our God is a person, full of feelings and emotions.

He is a person who feels happy and also gets angry. He laughs and cries. He is a person whom you can talk with, a person to whom you can explain things. He is One you can reason with, and who understands. He is reasonable, logical.

You can come to Him and say, "What about this situation?" And He will hear.

God is not a book full of rules. He is a person. He needs friends, and He is searching for friends.

A bishop from India said that he had been a very religious man before he was converted to Christianity. He had worshiped in every conceivable kind of temple. But he said that one word converted him to Christianity, and that word was "access."

He never found access to any of his gods in all of those temples, though they were myriad. He found access to God through Christ Jesus. The key idea of the New Testament is that we have access to God.

But we are too conscious of the Old Testament concept of God. "We come into Your presence," we say.

But God is tired of all that! He wants friends who will call Him *Abba*, "Daddy."

Once the Prince of Wales came to visit Argentina. When he arrived, we had all kinds of ceremonies. As he got off the plane there was the noise of the canon, and then music, and the formal greetings from government officials. I imagine that when he got into the hotel by himself he said, "Whew!"

The Prince of Wales saying that?

Of course. Do you think he lives in a tuxedo? He lives in pajamas, too—unless it is too hot. Yes, he gets tired of protocol.

I believe that God wants to fellowship with us when we are tired and sit with our shoes off or are relaxing in the bathtub. But we are too sophisticated. We have all of this protocol, and He is bored with it.

God is a person, inviting friendship. He wants to sit beside you and say, "Son or daughter, I love you."

He wants you to tell Him that you also love Him. He sent Jesus to earth for this very reason—to open access for us so that we could be His friends.

Actually, some of God's closest friends were not all that holy.

David was a man according to God's heart, but look at the things he did.

Abraham was the friend of God, and he did many things wrong. In fact, he was one of the worst ones! His father was a maker of idols, so he grew up in the worship of idols. He wasn't too good before God called him. But God made him His friend through grace, and purposed to bless the rest of mankind through him. It wasn't because Abraham was someone special, but because God needed him for His friend.

"You are going to be My precious friend, and through you a whole nation will be born who will also be My friends," God promised Him. "Although I am the God of all nations, I choose you to be close to Me and to bless the rest of mankind."

This is the real purpose of our friendship with God. It is not just to satisfy our ego so that we can say, "I am a friend of God."

God once went to Abraham's tent in the morning and spent the whole day with him. You read of it in the 18th chapter of Genesis.

God actually slept in Abraham's tent! How nice to have God sleeping in your tent. They talked, while Sarah prepared bread, and yogurt, and other dishes, with Abraham helping. God loves friendship. And before He left He gave Abraham the tremendous news of the coming of Isaac.

Imagine God coming to be with you the whole day! We preachers give five minutes to this and five minutes to that, but God spent the whole day in His friend's house just to give him the good news about Isaac. We see this of God's friendship throughout the Scriptures. He really takes an interest in His friends.

"Well, I have to leave," said God.

Then He thought to Himself, "I am going to destroy the neighboring cities of Sodom and Gomorrah because their sins are reaching up to heaven. Now these people are close to Abraham, but I haven't told him what I am going to do. I should tell him. What kind of friend is it that doesn't tell the other his secrets? I think I should tell him."

So he said, "Abraham, come."

"Yes, Lord, I am here."

"You are My friend. I have to share something with you. I am going to destroy Sodom and Gomorrah."

"But why?"

"Because their wickedness has reached up to heaven and we are tired of it all. They are bringing such terrible misery upon themselves, we have no option but to destroy them."

"Wait a moment," Abraham said. "I never knew this side of You. You are going to destroy these cities?"

"Yes, because of their wickedness."

"Are there not some just people living in those cities? Is everyone crooked? Are you going to destroy the just with the unjust? I can hardly believe that of a friend of mine!"

"Well, no—I don't want to destroy the just. So if there are 50 who are righteous in the city, I will not destroy it."

"Good. But what if there are only 45? Are you still going to destroy it?"

"Of course not. What do you think I am?"

"And suppose there aren't 45? What if there are only 40, or 30, Or 20? What if only 10 of them are righteous?"

"No, I won't destroy the city if there are just 10."

"Ah, that is better. I knew that You were really like this. You are wonderful."

"Thank you. But it is I who appreciate you because you reminded Me of this. We intended to destroy them all, we were so upset."

But there were not ten. The only righteous one was Lot. So when God arrived at the city He remembered Abraham's concern and took Lot and his family out of the city before He destroyed it. He did it for Abraham. What power there is in a friendship!

There are many instances of this in the Bible. God loves to have friends who remind Him of His nature, standing in the gap between God and man. This is what being a priest is all about, and it is tremendously important that we understand this in the times in which we are living.

13

Save Your Protocol for the President

The situation at the time of the flood was so terrible that God could stand it no longer. The whole earth had become corrupt, and violence was rampant. Every thought that men had was of how to do greater evil to one another.

So God determined to put an end to it all.

Noah was a friend of God. When God decided to destroy the whole earth, he was the priest to stand between God and man. A good priest doesn't use his influence to save himself. He has the rest of the world in mind. This is the reason he is chosen as a priest.

Whether Noah did all he could, we don't know. But at the end of 120 years of preaching, no one had been convinced. Perhaps he only preached against their sins, instead of showing them God's love, I don't know.

Following the flood, after God had expressed His full anger and was starting to cool down, He thought over what had happened on the earth.

"Look what I had to do!" He said to Himself. "Everything killed—the whole earth flooded. But they deserved it. I had the right to do it, because I created them and they sinned against Me."

After the water receded, Noah very innocently got out of the ark and built an altar. He took one of each of the animals

that God had designated as acceptable as sacrifices and of-
fered them on the altar.

Now, God was up in heaven saying to Himself, "Didn't I
do right? Look what they caused Me to do." Then He smell-
ed the sweet savor of Noah's offering.

"What is this sweet savor?" He asked the angels.

"It's Noah, from planet earth—the planet You just des-
troyed," they said.

"Noah? For Me? Look at that! Isn't that nice? I will never
destroy the earth again like that. I will not curse it again. I
will not let it rain that hard ever again, and I will put an arc in
the sky to remind Me when it rains that I should be careful."

This is the power of a priest. The ministry of priests is to
change attitudes—to change the attitude of man toward God,
and of God toward man.

It is a tremendous responsibility to be called as a priest. A
great many lives are dependent upon how we function in this
task. If we forget what it was like to be a sinner and begin to
judge and condemn people instead of loving them, we are like
Jonah. He was called as a priest, but he didn't do a very good
job.

Nineveh was a very sinful city. God told the prophet
Jonah, "Go and tell the Ninevites that I am going to destroy
them. I have had enough of their wickedness."

Jonah didn't want to go because he didn't care about all of
those people. Let God destroy them! So God had to persuade
him to go by means of a great fish.

Jonah should have done what Abraham did. But did he do
that? No, he was glad that the Ninevites were going to be des-
troyed. We need priests who, when they know that a calamity
is coming upon a city or a country, go before God and say,
"Please, no! Don't destroy them."

But Jonah's attitude was like that of some of us today, "So
You're going to destroy them? Well, they deserve it."

When God didn't destroy Nineveh, Jonah got upset.

"This is the very reason I didn't want to go there," he said. "I knew that You would forgive them if they were to repent!"

Instead of Jonah fulfilling the role of the priest, the heathen king of Nineveh became the city's intercessor. He stood in God's presence on behalf of the people and fasted.

"Look at that!" God said. "Look what he is doing! How can I destroy them?"

So Nineveh was spared.

One of the greatest intercessors was Moses. He really knew what it meant to be a priest. Do you recall the occasion when God became angry at the people, out in the wilderness?

"I can't stand it any more. I will destroy them and make a great nation out of you instead," he told Moses.

Moses wasn't interested in himself because he had the love of God. His total concern was for the people. He was willing to risk his own life to identify with them. He understood the principle behind Jesus' words when He said that if we really want to follow Him and be priests as He is our High Priest, we will be willing to take up a cross like He did and lay our lives down for others in order to show God's love for them.

So Moses answered God, "I will not get out of the way. If You destroy them, You will have to destroy me, too."

"What are you talking about, Moses?"

"I mean just what You heard. Take me out of Your book. The whole world is going to say, 'Look at their God. He took them out of Egypt to crush them in the wilderness. Look at that!' I won't stand by and let You do it."

"But Moses, you'll be all right. Just let Me destroy all of these wicked people, and I'll begin over again by starting a nation with you."

"Wait a moment! Cool down. This is not the way, to kill them all."

So Moses touched the heart of God, because God is not a

set of rules, a list of do's and don't's. He isn't One who condemns, and who can't be reasoned with. He is a person. You can talk to Him.

Jesus came in a human body like ours to be the greatest priest ever.

He lived on this earth, so He knows everything about being human. We do not have a High Priest who is unable to have compassion, because He went through all of the different experiences of being human that we go through. He also experienced the power of temptation. Because He understands, we can talk to Him. We can change God's attitude about a situation.

The reason we are not good priests today is because we don't know too much about friendship.

We have a religion instead of a relationship. If we had a relationship instead of all of our protocol, we would understand God's heart and know how to touch Him and change His attitude toward the people for whom we are called as priests.

What if I were to say to my wife, "Mrs. Ortiz, I come into your presence today..."? Our marriage would not last too long that way! And in the same way, God wants to enjoy the friendship that exists in a family. He is our Father. He is not a set of rules; He is a person.

This is not just a concept that I am giving you, it is a reality. I have experienced this wonderful fellowship with God personally. He really likes this kind of friendship, and He is looking for it.

People say to me, "But I like the protocol. I like the formality when I address God."

Yes, but what about what God likes?

Save your protocol for the President, or for the Queen, if you like it, but don't offer it to God. We are here to minister to Him, not to make ourselves feel nice by being very religious.

Our first child, David, slept all day, and cried all night.

After a few months, we were depressed and irritated because we couldn't sleep. So I said to Martha, "I am going to spank him, because he has to learn that the nighttime is for sleeping."

I turned the light on and I went to his bed. He was all smiles. "Goo, goo," he said.

"Look at this rascal," I said to Martha. "How can you spank a child that is smiling?"

God is a person with feelings. Noah, Abraham, Moses and many others changed God's attitude, just as I change my children's and my wife's attitude—and they know how to change mine when I am upset.

A priest is one who reconciles two parties. He has received the ministry of reconciliation, and his joy is to see two sides reconciled. There is nothing more important to him than this. He is willing to lay down his life to make it possible, just like Moses.

In New York City a pastor by the name of David Wilkerson opposed the police on behalf of some drug addicts. Everyone else was accusing them, but he was one man who was willing to fight for them. As a result, he won the love of those drug addicts.

But a priest has to be the friend of both sides. He cannot be one-sided.

So when we want to bring about reconciliation between a man and God, we first talk to one side.

"God, I understand. I am just like him. But because You created us, You have the right to do as You wish. Think it over. Perhaps He will accept You."

Then we say to God, "You know that we have been wicked from our youth. But You shed the blood of Jesus for the whole earth."

"Come on," we say to the man, "God will receive you."

"God, won't You take him in?"

We are in the middle, trying to make peace. So we have to

speak good of men to God, and good of God to men. But if
we act as gossips...“Look what they are doing! That’s terri-
ble!”...we are helping God to condemn people. We are no
better than Jonah. We are not suited to be priests.

Today, some prophets say that California is going to sink
into the sea. They are willing for that to happen so that their
prophecy is proved right. We don’t need those kind of
priests! Instead, we need priests who say, “No, God! Are
You going to sink the whole of that beautiful state?”

Do you think that you are going to please God by saying,
“Yes, God, destroy them all”? No, you will not please Him.
Because He will say to you, “And you, what did you do
about it? I sought for a man who would stand before Me for
the land that I should not destroy it, and where were you?”

God loves the world. I believe that every move God ever
made was a move of love.

He called Noah, Abraham, Moses and countless others to
stand in the gap between Himself and the people of the
world. He called them because He loved the world. He sent
His own Son into the world to be the great High Priest, to
stand as a friend of both sides. And He has placed you where
you are to be a priest, and to make His love known to those
around you.

The universal priesthood of the believer is one of the great
doctrines of the new covenant. Every believer is a priest. God
said, “Well, it failed with Israel, but with the church it is going to work. I’ll make them a kingdom of priests.”

We are here to stand between the world and God. But we
tell our ministers, “Please pray for me.” So this puts the
ministers between God and us. And what about those outside
the church? We have no time for them. We are centered on
ourselves instead of functioning as priests.

Ever since I was 14 years of age, I have been in the pulpit. I
grew up spending all my time with the holy nation. I was a

good church person. My fellowship was always with the professors of the seminary, or with pastors.

Then I discovered that I didn't know how to relate to the problems my people were facing in their factories and offices. So I decided to get a job in order to learn how to minister to them. I wanted to get in touch with their needs. I stayed in the pastorate, but I got a job as a part of my pastoral work, to see how my people lived.

The first day I was at work, they started to tell me all the blue and green jokes they knew. I never in all my life heard such things! I couldn't believe it.

On Monday morning everybody came to work to tell about all the dirty things they did on Saturday and Sunday—all the women they slept with, how they got drunk, everything that was ugly.

They brought pictures to the factory, and I said, "My goodness, is this where my people live? Then I am not ministering to them at all. I am telling them Bible stories about the millennium and the seven trumpets. They don't need that. They need to know how to face the situations they live in."

Many Christians are always saying with horror, "Look what that person is doing! Look what a wicked city this is! Lord, how can you spare them?"

God doesn't need those persons. Neither do we.

We are so afraid of being contaminated by the world. We forget that He who is in us is greater than he who is in the world. We have to love people and get in among them as Jesus did.

Jesus became our close relative. He became incarnate and dwelt among us. He didn't separate Himself from the world and put a sign up outside His house proclaiming, "Church of Jesus." He didn't expect the people to come to Him; He went to them.

On one occasion, He went to Matthew's house. It was full of publicans and sinners. "Look at that," the religious

*people said. "He can't be a prophet. He is in Matthew's
house, and it is full of sinners. Drugs, cards, prostitutes—doesn't He know what kind of people these are? If He
were a prophet, He would know about them and avoid
them."*

*But Jesus went anyway and told stories about the kingdom
of God because He didn't come to condemn, He came to
save.*

We are too holy. We are quick to forget what it was like to
be a sinner. So we go to the non-smoking side and let those
on the smoking side die!

To be priests, we have to be friends of both sides in order
to reconcile them. We have to become involved in people's
lives in order to bring them to God. This is what it is to be an
intercessor—to be one who stands between the two parties.

Paul wrote to Timothy, "First of all, then, I urge that en-
treaties and prayers, petitions and thanksgivings, be made on
behalf of all men, for kings and all who are in authority, in
order that we may lead a tranquil and quiet life in all godli-
ness and dignity. This is good and acceptable in the sight of
God our Savior, who desires all men to be saved and to come
to the knowledge of the truth" (I Timothy 2:1-4).

This is what pleases God—a love for all men. Not, "Oh
God, judge these terrible sinners."

God doesn't like that kind of prayer. He wants all men to
be saved. He must sorrow when He sees us so self-centered,
with concern just for ourselves.

"Alleluia, we are going to heaven!"

Yes. But what about everyone else? It displeases our Savior
when we have this attitude, because He wants everyone to go
to heaven.

"For God so loved the world," the Bible says. Let's
change that to read, "For we so love the world, that we
would do anything for them to be saved." This is what it
means to be a priest.

14

We Cannot Choose Our Brothers

I was at a church meeting once in which the pastor preached against smoking. He asked all the people who wanted to give up smoking to bring their cigarettes to the front.

It was very touching to see people bring their packets of cigarettes, their boxes of matches and their cigarette lighters, and throw them on the floor so that everyone could stamp on them and walk all over them. It made me especially glad to see young people there. What a testimony!

But sometimes I believe that we strain at a mosquito and swallow a camel. There are admonitions in the Bible that are much clearer than "thou shalt not smoke."

For instance, notice Jesus' prayer to His Father in John 17:20-23.

"I do not ask in behalf of these alone, but for those also who believe in Me through their word; that they may all be one; even as Thou, Father, art in Me, and I in Thee, that they also may be in Us; that the world may believe that Thou didst send Me. And the glory which Thou hast given Me I have given to them; that they may be one, just as We are one; I in them, and Thou in Me, that they may be perfected in unity, that the world may know that Thou didst send Me, and didst love them, even as Thou didst love Me."

Do you have any doubt that the Bible states clearly that the church is to be one? The Bible is absolutely clear in its revelation of the church as one—universally one.

But we are not one. Drive around sometime and see how many different church buildings there are in your community—maybe three or four.

These different buildings say, "We are divided." It would not be so bad if all of the different churches on a particular block used the same building at different times, putting their own sign up only when they were using the building. But we would not be happy with that.

The problem is, we think of sins only in terms of murder, theft, adultery or lying. We are horrified when someone commits adultery. We are even aghast at smoking cigarettes! We condemn the sins of the flesh, while ignoring the sins of the spirit. It is time we wake up to the fact that our division is very sinful from God's point of view.

Jesus' prayer was recorded because we were meant to hear it. In fact, we are accountable if it is not answered. It was recorded so that we could hear it and act on it. It is as if Jesus prayed it out loud in our midst. He meant it to be taken seriously.

When my children want something from me; they pray aloud.

"Lord, touch the heart of Daddy to take us to Disneyland." They mean me to hear their prayer because they want it answered.

Jesus prayed aloud so that His prayer might get into our Bibles, in all of our different languages. You know, it is in every Bible—the ones with the zippers and the ones without. It was said so loudly that everyone might understand the greatest and deepest desire of Jesus' heart. This is what His mind was on as He prepared to go to the cross. So it is very important that our minds are on it, too.

We are people who call ourselves Christians because Christ is the center of our message, the center of our lives, the center of our church system. He is the center of everything. That's why we have crosses all over the place—on our buildings, inside them, and on our person in many cases. We preach Christ, we pray to Christ, we praise Christ, we speak about Christ.

We had a tremendous expositor of the Gospels in our Bible seminary. She taught us, not just the letter, but the life of them. I recall the occasion when we came to the 17th chapter of John. She said, "This is the prayer of Jesus, so we are going to read this chapter on our knees." And we did.

Why is it that we do so little toward fulfilling this desire of Jesus if we love Him so deeply and preach about Him so much? Why is it that we don't act on His words, that His joy may be full?

Actually, those of us who are ministers are primarily responsible because we are the handles of the Christian community. We especially need to pay particular attention to Jesus' prayer. We may be good ministers of our various denominations; but when I was ordained, although I was ordained in a denomination, I was told that I was being ordained as a minister of the Lord Jesus Christ. So my allegiance, my loyalty, my commitment is first to Him, then to a denomination.

Now the church is universally one: There is just the one church in the whole world.

But that one church has its expressions in each locality. The church in Niagara Falls is the group of members who are part of this one universal church who also happen to live in Niagara Falls. The church in Buffalo is comprised of those members of the one church who happen to live in Buffalo.

This is the reason the Bible speaks of the church in Corinth, the church in Antioch, the church in Thessalonica, and so on.

The Bible is consistent in its revelation of these two dimensions of the church—the universal and the local. The problem today is that we have a third kind of church which is neither universal nor local. It is larger than the local church and smaller than the universal church. It is the denomination.

Now this creates a major problem for us, because there is no revelation in the Scriptures concerning the creation of a denomination. We can read the New Testament from cover to cover, but it isn't there.

What are we to do with our denominations? Well, we can't destroy them because they have become a way of life for us. Besides, those of us who see the vision for the church as Jesus meant it to be are usually not in a position to change the system. So the best thing we can do is simply to live as one church, as if our denominations did not exist.

The problem really isn't the denomination itself.

We are fooling ourselves if we believe that. We are the problem! The denomination is just another excuse for our flesh to become enmeshed in division, which it likes to do. It is an excuse for pride, jealousy and envy.

"They have a new pipe organ," says the number two church in the city. "We should get another, a larger one."

"They have lots of people," says the smaller church, "but they are not holy. We may be few, but at least we are holy."

Even in the same congregation we find division. There is rivalry among the deacons and elders. The problem is the flesh, not the system. The system is just one of the many avenues the flesh finds for expressing its divisiveness.

Most denominations begin in the same way. In a church, one group of people barks at another group, dividing over a particular issue. The other group then barks back. It takes two to fight. So we bark at one another, and division follows. Denominations are just an outgrowth of this division.

Martin Luther called the Pope the antichrist and the Catholic church the great harlot of the book of Revelation. No wonder he was excommunicated! We would be excommunicated from our denominations today for much less.

And so the Protestants divided from the Catholics. Then they divided among themselves many more times. Hundreds of denominations resulted.

I love Martin Luther. And I believe he played a very important part in the history of the church. But that doesn't make everything he did right. There was a mixture of flesh and Spirit, as there is with all of us. This is what creates the problems we have. Divisions are a work of the flesh.

It is the nature of the church that it is one. It cannot be other than one because it is the church of God, and God is one. Though there are Father, Son and Holy Spirit, God is one. It is His nature to be one.

Remember when Moses was called to deliver the children of Israel from Egypt? God spoke to him on the mountain out of a burning bush. He spoke his name, "Moses!"

"Who are You?" Moses asked. "Tell me Your name."

"My name?" answered God. He thought to Himself, "Poor Moses. He is used to so many gods and he thinks I am one of those gods. So He wants Me to give My name to identify Myself."

"Moses," He said, "I have no name."

"How come?"

"Because besides Me there is no god."

You know, we need names to identify one person from the other because we are many. Eve had to be given the name "Eve" because there was an Adam already. If Adam had remained alone, he would just have been himself without any need of a name.

"Come on, God, give me Your name."

"Moses, I tell you that I have no name."

"But I have to have a name!"

"Well, tell them that 'I am' sent you."

"I am what?"

"No, no. Just 'I am,' period. 'I am,' that's all. There is no other."

"But You can't ...."

"Moses, I am who I am. So go and tell them 'I am' sent you."

"What a funny name."

The first thing people ask me is, "Brother Ortiz, which church are you from?" I tell them that I am from *the* church.

"The church of what?"

"*The* church. *The* church, period."

"The period church?"

"No, no. Period isn't the name of the church. I mean *the* church."

Look in the Scriptures and tell me if you find a name for the church. It is just the church of God. The church is the church. It means the "called out" of God. It is composed of all who have been called out of the kingdom of darkness into the kingdom of God.

Are you called out? Then you belong to the same church that I belong to. By its nature, the church is one because we all have been called out of everything else into the kingdom of God.

Really, we shouldn't speak of the church as divided.

You can divide the number ten into ten ones, into two fives, or into five two's. You can divide a group of five into two groups (three and two) or into five ones. You also can divide two into two ones. But you cannot divide one. The church is one, and it cannot be divided. You can only break one.

When they amputate your leg, you don't say, "They divided my body." You say, "They cut off one of my legs."

So, too, the church is not divided; it is broken in pieces. And it is the job of the ministry to put the pieces together and to try to heal it so that it can function as one.

In the days of King Solomon, there were two women who each had a baby on the same evening. They were sleeping with their babies in bed and one turned over and crushed her baby. So while the other was still asleep, the one who had lost her baby stole the other woman's baby and put the dead child in bed with the mother.

Next morning, the woman found her baby dead and she recognized that her baby was the live one. No one had witnessed the exchange, so there was an argument. Each claimed the live baby was hers. So they brought the case to Solomon to judge.

"Both women claim the same baby," they told Solomon. "And there are no witnesses. We don't know what to do."

Solomon answered, "This is ridiculous. Divide the baby in two if both claim it is theirs. Bring me the baby and a sword, and we will divide it right now and give them half each."

The real mother said, "No, don't divide him. Give him all to her."

The other woman said, "Yes, divide him."

We have the same problem with people today. Some say, "Divide," when there are issues in which two parties disagree. Others say, "No." They understand that a body cannot be divided without killing it.

The trouble with the church today is that we have lost sight of the fact that there is a world to conquer.

The primitive church was just starting. It was small to begin with, but they conquered. Wherever they went, all over the earth, one desire consumed them: to bring the whole world into the worship of Christ. They preached Jesus, not a systematic theology.

The aim of the primitive church was not to have a bigger church, so that they could say, "Ours is larger than that one."

It wasn't to form separate denominations based on certain doctrines, calling themselves "Methodists" or "Presbyterians." No, their whole purpose was to expand the kingdom under Christ. They had unity because they were centered in Jesus.

Today we are not under Christ, but under other banners. So we have a broken church that is fractured into hundreds of denominations. But Jesus does not have many churches. The church is the bride of Christ, and He is not a polygamist. He is going to marry just one church.

Don't ask me which church I belong to, because there is

just *the* church. When you say "Baptist," "Methodist" or "Lutheran"...be careful. Those names are bad words in the kingdom of God. Don't repeat them too often, because Jesus may wash your mouth out with soap if you keep on saying those things.

We cannot choose our brothers. All the children of God in the same area belong to the same church, whether they like it or not. We cannot say, "You are my brother, but he is not my brother."

Who can choose his brothers in any family?

We are five in the family I was born into. I happen to be the last one. So when I was born, the other four were there. I didn't choose them, and they didn't choose me. When we were born, it was a fact that we were brothers.

Were we responsible for the fact that we were brothers? We did nothing to make ourselves brothers, nothing at all. The guilty ones were Mom and Dad. That my brother is my brother is not something I decided by myself; it is something I have to accept.

So it is in the spiritual family of God. You cannot pick out your brothers and sisters. You can select your friends perhaps, but not your brothers.

The church is formed of all those who have the Son within them. Whether they are Anglicans, Seventh Day Adventists, or Roman Catholics—if they have the Son, they are in the kingdom. They belong to the family of God. It's not by philosophical appoach, but by the life they have.

Jesus said, "I am the way, the truth, and the life." Our system of religion tells us that if we believe that Jesus is the way, that's okay. That's enough to be saved.

But it's not okay.

Jesus is not the way just so that we can believe that He is the way.

He is the way so that we can walk with Him. He is the truth not just so that I might believe that He is the truth, but that I may trust Him. And He is the life not just so that I can believe that He is the life, but that I might live that life. We cannot just have a doctrine or a concept, we must have the reality.

The primitive Christians were called those of "the way." Is the Anglican church the way? Are the Methodists or the Baptists the way?

No, the way is Jesus. It doesn't matter whether you are a member of a denomination or of an independent congregation. To be in "the way" is to have Him who is "the way."

If you are in Jesus, you are in the same way that I am. If you have the Son within you, you have the life of God.

It doesn't matter whether you believe in the millennium, or you don't believe in the millennium; whether you believe in the coming of Christ before or after the tribulation. Those things divide the people of God and have no value for living. They are just an intellectual approach to the philosophy of the Bible. They may be interesting, but they have nothing to do with whether or not we are brothers.

The church has a tendency to be a Christian club. A club is an institution in which all of the members agree to certain principles.

If we start a new club, say a non-smokers and non-drinkers club, it's because all of us agree not to smoke and not to drink. So non-smoking and non-drinking is what unites us.

If we start a single men's club, we are all single men. If you get married, "Out of the club!"

When we gather together around principles or doctrines, that's a club. Anything that is centered in a set of rules or concepts is a club. But when we gather together around a living person whose name is Jesus, we are a church.

In Argentina we have two big rival football clubs. They really are against each other. People come from all over the country to see their main matches. I went once, but I won't go again. I was almost killed.

When we get converted, we become Baptists or Espiscopalians. We are rivals. It's like two clubs. Before we fought for our politics or for our football club. Now we fight for our doctrines. But it's the same flesh finding new channels to manifest itself.

I used to belong to a church which prayed kneeling down. We never prayed standing or seated.

Once we went to visit another church where people stood to pray. We were scandalized. "Look at that! These cannot be Christians. They pray standing."

Today, the issue might be whether a brother is immersed or sprinkled in baptism, or whether he speaks in tongues or not. But all of these divisions are because we are more centered in doctrine and concepts than in life.

A person becomes your brother because he has been begotten by the Father.

I am your brother even if you don't like some of the things I am saying. I am sorry, but I cannot help it. I am your brother whether you accept the fact or not. Your acceptance doesn't make any difference. In fact, you had better accept me now because it might be that tomorrow, up there, the Lord will place my home beside yours!

Who knows whom the Lord will put in the same room of the same Holiday Inn in heaven? The Pentecostals and the Presbyterians together for eternity!! We had better get acquainted now. We had better accept each other now, regardless of our philosophies.

When Jesus comes to church, He does not find joy in our doctrinal divisions.

He commands us to repent of our hatred of one another. And when He lives within us and we are led by His Spirit, we will accept each other as members of His body not because of doctrines, but simply because He has accepted us. We will be one church because we all share one common life—the life of Christ in us.

15

Two Kinds of Wisdom

Do you believe that divisions are against God's will?

Of course you do. The Bible is very clear on that. And if they are against God's will, they are sin. Why don't we deal with the sin of disunity as we deal with other sins?

In many of our churches you can hear people say, "This brother is a heretic. If he doesn't leave, we'll have to throw him out." They insist that everyone should believe as they do.

But those who live in disunity—who do nothing to put an end to it—are the ones who should be ousted. Paul and the other New Testament authors are stronger in their denunciation of those who cause divisions than they are against any other form of sin.

We are very serious about the sins of the flesh. But when it comes to the divisions in the church, people say to me, "Brother Ortiz, you are off here. You are way out. You are too idealistic. Stop dreaming. Come back to reality. We have been divided all our lives, and you ask us to change now?"

We have become so used to divisions that we don't see them as a serious problem.

In the books of heaven they don't write the name of your denomination, they just write the names of people.

There isn't a separate book for the Baptists and another for the Methodists. I am sorry to have to tell you that they mix everyone up there...and you might be quite alarmed if you knew whose name appears next to yours! God could put Catholics and Pentecostals next to each other, and Baptists next to Methodists! I would like to see that book to discover whose name yours is written next to. The names are just by order of when you came into the church, not by denomination. Who knows whom you are next to?

The trouble is, we are so centered in doctrines that we cannot see beyond them. If Jesus were at the heart of our churches, we would be centered in life. Instead, we are centered in concepts.

So we excuse divisions by saying, "But there has to be a line somewhere."

In love, there is no fear. When we love, we do not have to be afraid of doctrinal differences because our emphasis is not on doctrine.

"God so loved the world." Not the Baptist doctrines, or the Presbyterian doctrines. "The world," with all of its erroneous concepts and terrible sins. Not when it was "right," but when it was in a lost condition. He came to a divided, confused, sinful world, and He loved it.

Many people are convinced that they have the right doctrines, but they are either naive or dishonest. How can you possibly be so sure that you have the right doctrines if you haven't been to the seminaries of the other denominations?

Let's say you are a Presbyterian. How can you be sure you have the right doctrine if you haven't been to the hundreds of other church seminaries?

In order to say that your doctrines are the right ones, you should go to them all and examine them carefully. It's not good enough to hear what they teach secondhand. You have to go to their seminaries and study them thoroughly before you can be so sure.

You have to go to the Catholics, the Lutherans, the Assemblies of God, the Seventh Day Adventists, the Baptists, the Methodists, the Nazarenes...and when you have finished studying all of them, if you haven't gone crazy you can decide which is the right one, or start a new one.

Without doing that, it is the height of arrogance to believe that you have all the right doctrines—and arrogance leads to divisions.

Actually, our seminaries do not teach the Bible as we claim they do. I was a professor in our seminary, and I have had to admit that we taught the doctrine of our denomination, and used the Bible to "prove" it.

If you go to a Pentecostal Bible school, they will teach you the Pentecostal doctrine and they will use the Bible to do so. If you go to a Seventh Day Adventist Bible school, what are they going to teach you? The Seventh Day Adventist doctrine! And what are they going to use to "prove" it? They will use the Bible. If you go to a Presbyterian seminary, you will find the same thing.

We can learn a tremendous lesson from the primitive church.

There were two churches—the church which was centered in Antioch, and the church which was centered in Jerusalem. They had different doctrines, because the church in Jerusalem consisted of Jews and the church at Antioch was made up largely of Gentiles.

The Jerusalem church believed in circumcision, keeping the law of Moses, worshiping in the temple, observing all the feasts of Israel, and living according to the customs and traditions of the Israelite law and culture. They even offered sacrifices in the temple! Actually, you remember that when Paul visited Jerusalem he shaved his head and sacrificed in the temple like any other Jew.

The only difference between the Jews in the church and all the other Jews was that the apostles and their disciples believed in Jesus Christ. And that was what saved them. They were correct Jews, plus they also believed in Christ. They were just like the other Jews except for the change in their attitude toward Christ. They said, "He is more than a prophet, He is the Son of God."

Now the church at Antioch was a very different church. Because they were Gentiles, they had no idea who Moses was. They knew nothing about the law or circumcision. Paul brought them to know Christ, not the Jewish religion.

Paul went into the wilderness following his conversion. He didn't begin to preach his Gospel to the Gentiles the day he was converted. He testified for a short time to Jews that Jesus is the Christ, but then went apart into a solitary place.

There were many years of darkness in his life when we don't know what happened to him. He was alone, perhaps ten years. During this time, God was at work on his mind. When he reappeared, he came with the understanding that the Gentiles could be wholly saved without accepting the Jewish system.

So he went to them and preached Christ crucified. That's all! They were Gentiles, fully saved, simply because they believed in Christ as their Savior and their life.

Christ is the reason they were saved, not Christ plus circumcision or any part of the law. Just Christ.

Problems came when some Jews went to visit the Gentile churches. The Jewish brethren believed that if these Gentile people had really received the Spirit, surely they would be circumcised and obedient to the law. They took it for granted that Paul had taught them all about the customs of Moses.

Consider what difficulties would have resulted if Paul had gone to the Gentile world and made them all first become Jews before they could receive Christ. What a task! That would have meant resting on entirely different days, eating different foods—living like Jews.

When a group arrived in Antioch to visit the church there, the Spirit was the same. There was the same love, joy, peace—the life was identical. They received the visitors from Jerusalem and held a great service of praise. They praised the Lord and sang in the Spirit, prophesied, and spoke in tongues. It was wonderful for Jews and Gentiles to worship together!

After the service the pastor said, "We can't let these brothers from Jerusalem stay in the Holiday Inn when we have lovely homes they could stay in."

So the Jewish believers were taken to the homes of the Gentile believers. Next morning the Gentiles said to their Jewish guests, "Listen, brothers. What would you like to eat? Would you like ham and eggs?"

"What?"

"Or perhaps you would prefer bacon?"

"What???"

"I said, 'Ham and eggs, or bacon and eggs?'"

"But that's unclean!"

"No, we are clean people. Come to the kitchen and see for yourself."

"No, no. I mean that ham is something Moses prohibited us from eating. He told us not to eat pork, ham or bacon. They are unclean."

"Moses? Who is Moses? He's never been to our church. We don't know that preacher."

"How ignorant! Don't tell me you don't know who Moses is? Why, surely you have been circumcised?"

"Circumcised? What is that?"

"Circumcision! Don't you know what circumcision is?"

"We never heard about circumcision. But if you want it for breakfast we can go to the supermarket to see if they have some."

"No, no. Circumcision isn't a breakfast food!

"Circumcision is what Abraham taught us to do. He circumcised Isaac his son, and Moses made it a central point of the law."

"Abraham? You are lucky in Jerusalem; you have all the preachers! Abraham has never been here."

What confusion! There was so much confusion that they had to have a general council in Jerusalem to settle the issue. Paul and several others had to journey all the way back to

Jerusalem from Asia to sort the problem out.

But we have a similar problem today. Some people say to me, "Is it true that Catholics have received the Holy Spirit?"

"Yes," I tell them, "many of them have become open to the Spirit."

"Wonderful. So they don't believe in the Virgin Mary or in the Pope any more?"

"Many of them believe in the Virgin as always, and in the Pope also."

"Oh, then it cannot be the Holy Spirit!"

"God knows their hearts—not you or I."

There are things which are essential and things which are not. The Christians from Jerusalem thought that because the Gentiles had received the Holy Spirit, they were now Jews. But Paul had learned what counts, and he had taught only Christ to the Gentiles.

We need to cleanse our message of salvation, freeing it from our doctrinal biases, if we ever are going to win the world. How can we convince people when the message we preach is different from church to church?

In one church you have to accept Christ plus the pipe organ, the hymn book, the liturgy, and the church board. If you go to a different church, you have to accept a set of doctrines, a different rite of baptism, and a different type of government.

If you are saved in a Baptist church, you have to accept democracy. If you are saved in an Episcopal church, you have to accept the bishop. If you are saved in a discipleship group, you have to accept submission and authority. Depending on the group, you have to accept Christ plus a system.

I believe that the essential is Christ in us. He is the One who is important. He in us is our only hope of glory.

Now, you and I cannot get all the churches together in unity, but we can bring an increasing consciousness of the horrendous situation in which we find ourselves.

I would like to suggest two things which every one of us can do to help end our divisions.

First, read what James says in the third chapter of his letter, verse 14.

"But if you have bitter jealousy and selfish ambition in your heart, do not be arrogant and so lie against the truth. This wisdom is not that which comes down from above, but is earthly, natural, demonic. For where jealousy and selfish ambition exist, there is disorder and every evil thing. But the wisdom from above is first pure, then peaceable, gentle, reasonable, full of mercy and good fruits, unwavering, without hypocrisy. And the seed whose fruit is righteousness is sown in peace by those who make peace."

There are two kinds of wisdom.

There is the wisdom that is earthly, unspiritual, demonic—the wisdom that appears so "right," but which causes strife and division.

Then there is the wisdom which comes from heaven—pure, loving, peacemaking, considerate, submissive, full of mercy, impartial and sincere.

Which is the wisdom you have? The one which causes divisions, or the one which produces peace?

So I suggest, first of all, that we never speak against any other group again. Never again! Say, "Lord, I will not open this mouth of mine to speak against any other church." If we cannot have an active part in bringing about unity, we can certainly play a passive role by shutting our mouths. This will foster peace.

Second, let us love those who do not think as we do. We know that they love Christ—and it is not a question of whether they love us, but of whether they love Christ. I do not travel around the world to try to get people to love me, but to get them to love the Lord. So if you love Him, you are my brother. We are one in Christ.

Let us consider our different religious denominations as if they did not exist. Go to the Baptist convention, or to the Assemblies convention, if you have opportunity, as if there were no differences. Go to your own fellowship and be faithful to it, but ignore the divisive elements. For you and me, they are not there. They are there for those who practice the false wisdom, but not for us; so we can ignore them.

Once I was taken to a beautiful Baptist church. They didn't say "praise the Lord" there, but I was able to enjoy their wonderful building.

When I hear that the Catholics are building a new building I say, "Wonderful, praise the Lord! *We* have another building."

Paul said that the whole world is ours. Whether it is Paul, Peter, Apollos—all are ours. If you choose Paul, you have only the one person. If you don't choose one, you have all of them. Do you understand? If you choose, you have only the Presbyterians or the Baptists. If you don't choose, they are all yours. You can learn from the rich heritage in each of them ignoring the divisions.

But you say, "How can I accept someone when I believe that his doctrines are completely wrong?"

Our problem is that our basis for acceptance is wrong. It is the same basis the world has, whereas it ought to be the same basis that God has for accepting us.

Does God accept us because we are nice, because we have good character, or because we are extroverted? Does He accept us because we have what we believe are the right doctrines? Does He accept us because we do all kinds of good works?

No, He accepts us because of the blood of Christ.

When we get to heaven the song will not be, "We are up here because we believe in the millennium, and we have the right theology on the Trinity." It is going to be, "We are here because of the blood of the Lamb." He is going to be the One we will glory in, not the theology which defined the doctrines.

We are going to spend eternity with God because of the blood of Jesus, not because of the theology of Luther, Calvin, or Wesley; not because of what was taught in Princeton, Dallas, or Pasadena.

If God accepts me because of the blood of Jesus, who are you to look at me on another basis, in the manner the world does? If you love those who love you, and whom you agree with, are you any different from the world?

God loves me because my sins, my mistakes, my errors, my failings have all been forgiven through the blood of Jesus. So I love you because your sins and faults have been forgiven also.

I once heard a tremendous sermon on how the righteousness of God covers us like a new coat. But I wonder how it can be that God sees us in that coat, yet we cannot see each other in it? If the coat is good enough for God, how come it is not good enough for us?

I see you dressed in the righteousness of God. Now, put that coat over the dress of your denomination. Put God's uniform on. Because at the marriage supper of the Lamb, He provides the wedding garments—we don't bring our own. And He isn't going to ask, "How many are from this denomination, and how many are from that denomination?" He isn't interested in our denominational dress, just in the dress He gives us.

In the parable Jesus told about a king who made a great feast for the wedding of his son, those who were invited wouldn't come. So the king became angry and said, "Kill them all!" Then he said, "The feast is ready. The meat is all succulently roasted. The Coca Cola is chilled. Go and invite everybody—the sick, the lame, the beggars, anyone who will come."

So the servants went out and they saw a beggar. "Hey, you, the king has invited you to the wedding of his son."

"The king? Invited me? You're crazy."

"Yes, you. You are invited."

Everybody was invited. They couldn't believe it, but they

decided to come anyway. One young man was different.

"Has the king invited me?"

"Yes, you too."

"Ah, I always believed I was somebody," he said to himself. So he went to his house and found the best suit he had, ironed it, combed his hair, and doused himself with Brute. But when he arrived at the wedding and was about to enter they said, "Wait a minute. Where are you going?"

"I'm going to the wedding."

"But you have to go to that room over there to receive the dress the king has provided you with for the wedding."

"I don't need any dress. I have my own suit on."

"I am sorry, but this kind of wedding you have to have the garment prepared by the king."

"These are my very best clothes, and they are better than anyone else's. I'll wear what I am wearing now."

So he went in, and he saw that everyone was dressed in fine linen, and beautiful brocade. His clothes looked like filthy rags by comparison. He felt a mess.

"This is horrible! What shall I do?"

He tried to hide himself, but that was impossible. He stood out like a sore thumb, and you know, he was thrown out.

Which dress do you have on?

Be careful....you had better take the dress the king provides. It is the righteousness of Jesus Christ that counts, not your doctrines or the name of your denomination. We are righteous not because of ourselves, not because we belong to a particular denomination, but solely because of the blood of Jesus.

"Forgive us our trespasses," we pray, "as we forgive those who trespass against us."

We are forgiven on the same basis that we are to forgive. And what is that basis? The blood of the Lamb. We are forgiven because of Jesus' shed blood. And we forgive others because they also are under the blood.

The Father accepts me because of the blood of Jesus, through grace.

It has nothing to do with what I do or what I think. He has forgiven me because of Jesus. And you have to accept me for the same reason. This means that you forgive me all my wrong doctrines, and I forgive you. I forgive you if you are an Episcopalian, a Baptist, or a Lutheran. You are forgiven, as I am!

When Jesus comes to church—when He is the focus of our attention—we cannot help but love each other and accept each other.

Division and disunity are the result of adding something to just simply faith in Jesus. But when He is the center of our lives, we will be one church as He intended. And the world will see, by our love for one another, that Jesus really is alive today.

16

Why Does God Love Us?

Many of us find it very difficult to love other people.

But love is a command for the Christian. It is not an option; it is an order. Jesus said, "A new commandment I give to you, that you love one another, even as I have loved you, that you also love one another" (John 13:34).

One of the reasons we have difficulty loving others is because we do not really know the depth of God's love for us.

So we are going to take a look at how God loves us. When we discover how He loves us, we will learn how to love others. We are to love with the same kind of love He has for us.

There are many passages of Scripture we could turn to in order to understand God's love for us, but I want to use one which has been very meaningful in my own life. It is Colossians 2:13-14.

"And when you were dead in your transgressions and the uncircumcision of your flesh, He made you alive together with Him, having forgiven us all our transgressions, having cancelled out the certificate of debt consisting of decrees against us; and He has taken it out of the way, having nailed it to the cross."

Do you know when God started loving you?

"When you were dead."...What a time to start!

The most helpless and unattractive phase of a human being's life is a horrible stink. Moreover, we were not only dead; we were dead in our transgressions. So this is not a picture of a dead person lying in a nice casket, draped in silk: this is a dead corpse in the mire, lying in all of the filth.

But even when we were so unattractive, God loved us.

He didn't love a nice looking person who carried a Bible under his arm and a cassette recorder in his hand. He loved a dead corpse in all of its filth.

I asked myself once, "Why does God love us?" A great many people have puzzled over that question. Now I believe I understand the reason. *It is because He made us, and we are His children.*

If you have children, are they perfect? Do they never disobey? Are they always clean and tidy? No, of course not.

So why do you love them?

You love them because they are your children. Sometimes they do some very wrong things, but you still love them. They dump their milk on the carpet, write on the walls, cry at night, misbehave when you have visitors...but you love them anyway.

There's no mystery about your love for them—you love them because you can't help loving them. So don't be surprised that God loves you. You belong to Him. And, in spite of everything, He loves you.

Once you realize that God loves you just as you are, you begin to relax.

To know that you are accepted and loved just as you are takes all the tension out of your relationship with Him.

This is how we are to love one another—just as we are. We should love one another not because the other person is good, right, or nice, but just because we are brothers.

God loves us because He made us and we are His. We should love one another just because we are people, not because of desirable qualities. If God took into account our behavior, our works, our ways or our doctrines, He would hate us! But He loves us because we are His creatures. And we are all brothers and sisters in the same created family.

He also loves us because He gave us life.

If you had a son or daughter who died and you had the power to raise that son or daughter up, wouldn't you do it? Of course you would. Then don't wonder that God did it, because He had the power. When we were dead, He gave us life because we are His children.

Do you ever get upset with your kids? Most of us do.

God also gets upset with us. One time He got so upset with His children that He sent a flood that swept most of them away. He repented that He had made them.

I have seen that happen with some parents, after their children have been apprehended by the police because they were using drugs and stole in order to pay for their habit.

"I'm sorry I ever had children," I have heard them say. But later on, they see their children in another light. Then they no longer are sorry that they gave birth to them.

The same is true of God.

Another day, God sent a second flood. This flood solved His problem with His children once and for all.

The second flood was the blood that flowed from Jesus on the cross. God's plan was to put everybody on that cross in Christ. So much so that Paul said, "I have been crucified with Christ; and it is no longer I who live" (Galatians 2:20). And again in II Corinthians 5:14, "One died for all, therefore all died."

Jesus did not die for Himself because He didn't need to die and be born all over again. He didn't need to be saved; He had no sins to pay for because He was born and lived without sin. He was born of a virgin so that Adam's sin did not affect Him. Therefore, He could be the spotless Lamb of God. If He had been a sinner Himself, He could not have paid for our sins. His death was for us, not for Himself.

The cross was a common mode of execution. The Romans killed tens of thousands on crosses. Many of them died innocently, as martyrs. What made the difference with Jesus' death was that from the Father's point of view it was not really His Son dying there, it was you and I.

That's why He turned His back on His own Son: He had become identified with the entirety of the human race. He has become sin personified. He who was without sin was made sin for us.

Jesus voluntarily took our place, taking upon Himself our sinful state. In God's eyes He was guilty, though He Himself was innocent.

It is very important that we understand this. Because if you look at the cross and see Jesus hanging there with thorns pressed into His scalp and blood dripping from Him, and you say, "Poor Jesus!" you are looking only at a martyr.

But if you look at the cross and by faith see hanging there what God put on the cross, you see yourself. And when you see yourself on the cross, Jesus becomes your Savior.

You were the problem that God wanted to do away with!

And this time, no one was left out—not even Noah. From the first human being in the garden of Eden to the last person who is not yet born, all were put on that cross. You and I were not yet born when the cross happened, but we were there because it takes in the entire fallen race of mankind. This is the second flood, in which God finished with everybody.

When Jesus said, "It is finished," He meant that Juan Carlos Ortiz was finished. That was my problem—Juan Carlos Ortiz. But God finished with that problem by killing me on the cross.

He finished with your biggest problem too!

But not only were we in Christ when He died, we were in Christ when He rose. This is what our baptism pictures.

The problem is, many of us don't understand what baptism means. We sometimes try to create an emotional experience out of it because we believe that we have to feel something in order to be born again. Even some preachers try to create the kind of atmosphere which stirs up our emotions to the point that we weep, thinking that this is evidence of our new birth.

But this is completely erroneous. In fact, I prefer a dry-eyed born again person to a wet-eyed one, because the one who doesn't get too emotional perhaps understands better what has happened to him.

Our baptism declares that when Jesus died, we believe that we too were crucified and buried with Him. He also experienced resurrection. In our case, we don't have to experience crucifixion, burial and resurrection: we just believe what already happened in Christ.

If God says it, we believe it; we don't have to look to feelings. When those who base their faith on feelings don't have those feelings, they may not have faith either. But when we base our faith on facts, the facts never change.

You don't say, "I feel today that Washington was the first president of the U.S."

The fact of his presidency has nothing whatever to do with your feelings.

Neither do you say, "I feel today is Tuesday." Whether you feel it or not, it is Tuesday.

To base our faith on feelings is to build on a shaky foundation of sand. To base our faith on the facts of what God tells us happened to us in Christ is to build on a solid foundation which will never move.

From God's viewpoint, we have been put on the cross—we are in Christ.

Paul puts this very simply when he describes, in Romans Chapter 5, two heads of two different races. Adam was the head of the physical human race; Christ, the Second Adam, was the head of a new race. Under Adam we all were made sinners, but under Christ we all are made righteous.

The whole human race was included under Adam. In the same way, all who believe in Him are included in Christ.

From the very first human being who walked the earth to

the last who will ever live, all were declared sinners because of Adam—and all are declared righteous because of Christ. When Jesus died, the Scriptures say that He descended into the depths of the earth and preached to those who died before the cross ever happened. That means the cross was effective for the whole human race.

For the sin of Adam, I am declared a sinner; for the righteousness of Jesus, I am declared righteous by faith.

The point I want to emphasize is that I became a sinner through no cause of my own, so also I become righteous through no cause of my own. This is something that God does.

"When we were dead, He gave us life." A dead man cannot help himself.

We should have no difficulty understanding that we were born sinners, because from the very beginning we started to disobey.

One of the earliest things I learned to say was, "No!" So did you. No child ever said, "Yes, Mommy; of course, you are right." We are born rebellious, born crooked.

But the Bible says, "Therefore if any man is in Christ, he is a new creature; the old things passed away; behold, new things have come" (II Corinthians 5:17).

When we believe in Christ, we become part of a new humanity. What He accomplished in His death and resurrection becomes a reality to us simply through believing. The instant we believe, we start life all over again—the old person is dead and a new person has come into being.

Now let us see what our death means.

Paul goes on to say in the passage we are looking at from Colossians, "Having forgiven us all our transgressions." Having forgiven us how many? All!

Do you know what all means? The *all* of God is different from your all and my all.

If I tell someone, "Brother, I forgive you all that you did

against me," although I don't say it, it is understood that I forgive him all that I know about.

If tomorrow I discover some other terrible thing that he did, I'll challenge him again, "And what about this also?"

When God says all, He knows everything. His all is greater than our all. He knows every detail of every sin we have ever committed, far more than we ourselves know.

Also, it is evident that when I say, "I forgive you all," I mean all until the present moment. But from now on, beware! Whereas in the case of God, He knows the future. When He saved us, He knew the problem He was getting into. He knew everything about us from the beginning to the end of our lives.

God is an eternal Being. For an eternal Person there is no past or future: everything is in the present.

Because we are limited, we have past and future as well as the present. But God sees everything in the present. That is why He can take something that is going to happen a thousand years from now and show it to you in a vision or through prophecy.

God doesn't have to wait until the end of the year to balance His business as you and I do; He can do His bookkeeping before the year begins. He knows everything in advance—in advance for you and me, but not for Him; because for Him there is no advance. He doesn't live in days and nights: a thousand years is like one day.

Einstein said that if we were to travel at the speed of light, we could live in the present continually. But God is the father of light, the creator of it, the One who said, "Let there be light." He lives in another dimension where time doesn't count.

God, of course, is the only one who lives in the present.

We don't know the present: we have only past and future. Perfect present doesn't exist for us. When I say, "I am in the present," as I say the word present it is already past. When I say "sent," "pre" is past. In order to have perfect present, we would need to stop the time, and in the dimension we live in we cannot do that.

So the present is the prerogative of God.

For God there is no future. His name is, "I am." His very name speaks of the eternal present. Jesus also said, "Before Abraham was, I am."

Because we live in the dimension of time we would argue, "Lord, you don't know grammar. You should say, 'Before Abraham was, I was.'"

"No sir, I am."

"But before Abraham was is past, so you have to say, 'I was.'"

"What do you mean, 'Past'?"

You see, for God there is no time. Everything is perfect present. That is why Jesus also said, "Lo, I am with you always, even to the end of the age." He didn't say, "I will be with you." He said, "I am." The Bible describes us as seated in the heavenlies.

"Lord, what a mistake. You mean we will be *seated, in the future; because we are not yet seated."*

"No, I mean you are *seated, present tense."*

We are also spoken of as predestined, called, and justified—all of which we can agree with. But then it says, "Glorified."

"Glorified? No, not yet."

"Yes, now. Glorified."

"How can You say that, Lord?"

God lives in the eternal realm of which we are not conscious in our natural state. But the eternal realm is more real that the "real" world around us.

When we die, we lose our present consciousness of time and space and enter into God's dimension. In this dimension, Jesus is the Lamb of God offered before the foundation of the world, because for Him there is no time other than the perfect present.

Do you believe that Jesus took your sins away when He died on the cross? Of course you do. But since you were not yet born, how could He have done that? How could He pay for sins which you hadn't even committed?

Because He lives in the present, God knew all your sins before you committed them in the dimension of time and space. He knew them all. Do you think that you are going to commit a sin one of these days which is going to take God by surprise?

Can you imagine Him saying, "Oh my, I forgot to put that one on the cross!"

No, that can't happen; you can't take the eternal I Am by surprise.

If God has called you, relax. He knew whom He called. He knew everything about you from the beginning of your life to the end. And He forgave you all your transgressions.

One day I had a revelation of the meaning of this word *all* in my own life.

For many, many years I had very bad migraine headaches. Do you know what a migraine is like? Those who don't have them don't know. It's like those who are single who think they know how to rear children: even if they have learned about such things in school, they don't know. A migraine is terrible.

I used to have them two or three times every week. They started at about 5:30 in the morning with a little pain in my forehead, spreading to the area of my eye, with accompanying symptoms of nausea, an increased pulse and frequent fainting. There were times when I was driven to distraction; I couldn't stay locked in my room in darkness. So I would go out, and faint.

Three times I fainted in the pulpit and was taken to the hospital.

Needless to say, I went to the best doctors in Argentina,

North America and Europe. I had friends in the church who were doctors, and they did what they could for me. In the end they sent me to a psychiatrist. He prescribed valium. I took it for a time, until I decided that I shouldn't do so any longer. But the migraines kept coming, continually worse.

Not long after I wrote the book *Disciple,* I was at home studying this passage in Colossians 2 for my personal benefit.

I said, "Lord, does this mean that you have forgiven me even for the things I haven't done yet? Then that means that you accept me just as I am!"

God seemed to answer me by saying, "You are the preacher, and you don't know that? Stupid!"

Actually, I had preached it; I was professor of Romans in our seminary. But though I knew it in my head, it had not yet dropped down to my heart. I understood that I have peace with God not through my performance, but through Jesus; I hadn't yet seen that the only way to have peace with myself is also through Jesus and not through performance.

That day the Holy Spirit continued to talk to me. "Do you know what your problem is, Juan Carlos?" He asked me. "You haven't accepted yourself as you are."

"Wait a minute," I interjected. "How can I accept myself as I am knowing myself as I do? I can't possibly accept myself. Actually, I am very upset with how I am doing. My character is very poor. No, I can't accept myself!"

The Lord seemed to get a little upset with me.

"If the blood of Jesus My Son is good enough for Me, who are you for it not to be good enough for you?" He challenged. "Are you better than I?"

I began to see that acceptance has nothing to do with performance. No matter how bad I am, the blood of Jesus is sufficient. And if God had forgiven me and accepted me such as I was, then I had better accept myself.

"You know, Juan Carlos," the Lord continued, "I know you better than you know yourself. Actually, you are worse

than you think. But I have accepted you—not because of your performance, but because of the blood of Jesus. Although I know all your wrongs, I have forgiven them all, right up until the day you die. Unless you forgive yourself all your wrongs—not just some of them, but all—and unless you promise yourself that you are always going to forgive yourself, you will never have peace with yourself."

Do you know where inner peace comes from? It comes from accepting yourself.

Do you know why we have problems with the people around us? All of the problems we have with people around us are a reflection of the problems we have within ourselves. And the problems we have within ourselves are a reflection of our lack of faith that our problem with God is completely and forever solved.

How rightly the hymn says, "My faith is built on nothing less than Jesus' blood and righteousness; all other ground is sinking sand." I don't look any more to my performance, I look to what God looks at—the blood of Jesus.

That day I said to myself, "Johnny Ortiz, forgive me. I was so rough with you. I struck blows at you. I even hated you sometimes. I was like a masochist. I was forever trying to condemn you. No wonder you wept and experienced depression and insomnia. But now I am sorry. Juan Carlos, I forgive you everything past, present, and even in the future. You are fully forgiven."

So I hugged Juan Carlos, and we went to bed together and fell asleep very quickly.

Three weeks later I said, "Where are my migraines?"

Several years have gone by now, and I have not had one migraine!

When I made peace with myself, they ceased completely.

Do you know why we sometimes don't receive healing? Because we don't deal with the cause, which is our lack of peace.

I had gone to doctors, but also to many faith healers. Every one of them I came in contact with, I asked for prayer. There were some big names among them. But nothing happened.

Suppose you have a nail in your shoe which is hurting your foot. You limp around in great pain, begging everyone, "Brother, please pray for my foot!"

And although one after the other prays, nothing happens. What is the answer? You have to take the nail out. Isn't that simple?

No wonder the Bible says that "the chastening for our well-being fell upon Him, and by His scourging we are healed." The word well-being is translated "peace" in the King James Version. Our health is directly affected by our inner sense of peace. Jesus takes the nail out of the shoe!

No amount of prayer or visits to doctors could heal me. My problem was my lack of acceptance of myself. So the very day I accepted myself, my migraines were finished. I forgave myself all my trespasses, just as God had forgiven me.

And when I found peace, I found health also.

17

Yes, But I Love You

When some people hear that we have been forgiven all our sins they ask, "Well, if the Lord already has forgiven me everything, and if even the sins I haven't committed yet have been taken care of, why should I try so hard not to sin?"

Actually, they have a good point. God never meant us to fret and worry about whether or not we might sin.

When Paul dealt with this same question, he implied that we would have to be stupid to think that a person who died to sin could keep on living in it. He did not say, "Oh, be careful! That's dangerous. You had better really try hard not to fall into sin."

No. He said, "It is impossible for one who is dead to continue in sin."

The grace of God has two dimensions.

One dimension is the forgiveness of all our sins.

The other dimension is, "I will give you a new heart and put a new spirit within you; and I will remove the heart of stone from your flesh and give you a heart of flesh. And I will put My Spirit within you and cause you to walk in My statutes, and you will be careful to observe My ordinances" (Ezekiel 36:26-27).

We receive the Holy Spirit, and the fruit of the Spirit is love, joy, peace, longsuffering, gentleness, goodness, faith, meekness, self-control, and "against such things there is no law'' (Galatians 5:22-23).

Therefore, one who has the new heart doesn't need any law because the Holy Spirit makes the law unnecessary. This is why Jesus said that all the law and the prophets are fulfilled in one word, love.

Paul explained, "For this, 'You shall not commit adultery, you shall not murder, you shall not steal, you shall not covet,' and if there is any other commandment, it is summed up in this saying, 'You shall love your neighbor as yourself.' Love does no wrong to a neighbor; love therefore is the fulfillment of the law'' (Romans 13:9-10).

The fruit of the Spirit causes us to do what the law aimed at, plus a great deal more. This makes the law unnecessary.

We receive a new heart to live in holiness, and to produce all of the fruit of the Spirit. We also have the forgiveness provided for in the blood of Jesus to be sure that we never never, never lose this salvation that God has given us.

Have you ever been to a circus, or seen one on television?

One of the most spectacular acts is the trapeze. It is breathtaking to watch the performers swing from one bar to another, because they are so high up in the top of the tent. They throw one person to another, and you wonder, "What happens if they fall?"

Once I asked one of them, "How are you able to perform so perfectly? You never fall."

"Yes, we fall," this performer explained. "We fall in almost every show."

"But I have never seen you fall."

"Well, you saw us fall, but you didn't notice it because we learn how to fall and recover. When we fall we jump back up quickly and people think it is part of the show."

God gave us a new heart and the Holy Spirit so that we may live in the Spirit—like a trapeze performer on the trapeze.

We should be a display to all the world, especially to our neighbors, so that they say, "Look at those people. Look how they love one another. They never criticize anybody.

They love even their enemies. They are the best neighbors. No one has any complaint about them. And they are the best workers in the factory, the most loyal secretaries, the best lawyers. See how lovely their wives are, and how obedient their children are."

Of course, we are not yet perfect. But when we are living in the Spirit we can recover quickly because it is the life of Jesus that people see—not us.

If we slip and fall, there is a net underneath. The blood of our Lord Jesus Christ has provided forgiveness for all our failures. If we fall a thousand times, a thousand times He will push us up so long as our honest desire is to be up.

Now if you fall, then go to sleep on the net, I wonder if you would last in the circus. You would be an unprofitable performer.

But if you really want to live in holiness—to live (even fall and recover) on the trapeze—you need to know that there is a net underneath.

The trapezists can be relaxed because they know there is a net. If there were no net, they would be tense and afraid.

When we are tense and afraid, it is more likely that we will fall.

Those who are afraid to fall find that they fall continually.

Those who try hardest to live in holiness find that it is difficult to do so.

But those of us who aren't struggling to live in holiness are so relaxed that we are living in holiness! Because holiness is not something that comes from our own efforts, it is a gift of God—the Holy Spirit in us doing the work of Jesus.

Praise the Lord for His wonderful love! He forgave us all our trespasses; He provided us with a net so that we can relax. And He tells us to love one another as He has loved us.

Are we prepared to do that? Or do we try to pull the net out from under our brother? If he falls, "Bye, bye." We reject him forever!

Why is it impossible for one who is truly in Christ to continue in a life of sin? Simply because Jesus dealt with the root of our problem. You and I are the roots of our problem; and when Jesus died on the cross, we also died with Him. It was not only our sins that were nailed to the cross, it was ourselves!

Now, because He had dealt with our problem He was able to do something else. The book of Colossians goes on to say that He "cancelled out the certificate of debt consisting of decrees against us and which was hostile to us; and He has taken it out of the way, having nailed it to the cross."

There is a file in heaven for every individual who ever has lived. We don't know how God does His bookkeeping. But in the days in which the Bible was written, they spoke of God keeping His accounts in books.

On the first page of my file it says, "Juan Carlos Ortiz...6,276 hairs on his head, etc."—all of the details so that there is no question who it is.

On the second page all of God's laws are written, especially the Ten Commandments. Next, pages are provided to register every time I transgress each commandment. My file is very thick!

On the last page is the certificate of debt.

It reads, "Because Juan Carlos Ortiz has transgressed the first commandment 8,322 times, the second 5,456 times, the third...the fourth...therefore Juan Carlos Ortiz goes right into hell."

Because I died with Him, Jesus got out my file, took a big rubber stamp and wet it in His blood, and stamped "cancelled" on every page of the file. Then He took that file out of the way because He didn't want that garbage in heaven. So no one else could ever see it, the surest place He could find was to nail it to His cross. If anyone wants to see Johnny Ortiz's file, they have to pass over Jesus' dead body!

So now God goes to the files of heaven and says, "Let me see Johnny Ortiz's file. Why, it's not even here...There's nothing at all against him. What a servant I have!"

Praise the Lord, this is the way He loves you and me. Now we have perfect peace with God. But although we sing these things in our hymn books and preach them from the pulpit, many of us do not live as though this were a reality. We sing, "I had a debt I could not pay..." and we live as if we still had that debt! We don't believe we are fully accepted.

People come to me and say, "Pastor Ortiz, could you pray for my husband?"

"Why don't you pray?" I ask.

"Oh no, the Lord hears you better. You are so saintly."

What does a person mean when he tells his pastor that the Lord hears him better? He means that perhaps he is not as accepted. This is because we put our trust in our behavior, in our performance.

Satan knows how easily we feel condemned, so he is quick to get us to look at our works. But if the Lord were to judge us by our performance, we would all be lost! It is because of the blood of Jesus that He accepts us.

In order to trick us, before Jesus raided the files of heaven Satan made photocopies. Of course, they are invalid; but he uses them to fool us.

He doesn't fool me any more. But be careful; he fools many people. Satan takes my file and shows it to you, and takes your file and shows it to me, trying to get us to judge each other.

Oh, Satan is so smart. He tried to make even Jesus doubt. "If You are the Son of God..." he kept saying.

He tries to sow a slight doubt in the back of our minds that perhaps God doesn't accept us as we have heard preached.

Once I accepted myself and forgave myself all my sins, as God had forgiven me, the Lord showed me that I was to accept my brothers and sisters as they are and forgive them all their sins, too.

I was learning the meaning of Jesus' words, "Forgive us our trespasses, as we forgive those who trespass against us."

"Lord, how many times shall I forgive my brother if he trespasses against me?" someone asked Jesus.

His answer was 70 times 7, which is 490. From sunrise to sunset on an average day, that is one time every minute-and-a half. That is a full-time job. And some students say that Jesus meant 7 to the power of 70, which is 2 numbers plus 54 zeroes!

If you forgave once every second, to forgive that many times you would need to live millions of years. Do you see how big "all" is? It means that we forgive every time.

Therefore, I have to accept my sister not because of her behavior, not because of her doctrine, but by the blood of Jesus. And I accept her because I forgive her all her sins.

Do you see how unity has been guaranteed by the cross?

On the cross, Jesus cancelled out everyone's debt. So when we accuse a brother or sister, we are accusing people whose debt already has been cancelled out. We are wasting our time finding fault with others. We who are true believers are all going to be in heaven together because of Jesus, so we had better begin to accept each other now, just as we are.

When I forgave myself all my sins and accepted myself, I slept soundly that night. When I woke up the next morning the Lord explained that I needed to accept other people on the same basis as He had accepted me and I had accepted myself.

So the first person I accepted just as she is was my wife.

When you fall in love, you want to get married so that you are together. The person you love is the most wonderful person in the world. So you get married, and you go on the honeymoon.

But when you get back from the honeymoon you say, "Well, she will change—we have only just got married."

While you are thinking that she will change, she is saying to herself, "I hope he will change."

But after you pass 40, she says, "He won't change!" And you also realize that since she hasn't changed yet, she isn't going to change either. That's why you have to learn to accept one another as you are.

Not only are we one in a marriage, we are one church as believers. We are all collectively one. And our oneness is based on the guaranteed forgiveness of all our sins. No wonder Paul said, "Who shall separate us from the love of Christ?" Who shall accuse the chosen of God? Who will condemn us? What an assurance... "Blessed assurance."

Since I came to understand this, I began to sing some of the words of our hymns in a new way.

I used to sing, "Amazing grace, how sweet the sound, that saved a wretch like me...." Now I have learned to sing, "Amazing grace, how sweet the sound, that saved a wretch like *him*. 'Twas grace that brought *him* safe thus far, and grace will lead *him* on."

I also used to sing, "Just as I am, without one plea...." Now I have learned, "Just as *he* is, without one plea...."

So I would like to give you some homework. You could do this with many passages, but begin with Ephesians chapter one.

Whenever we read this passage we each think of it as being for ourselves. But I would like you to think of it as being for someone else. I believe this will introduce you to a new dimension in your relationship with other Christians, just as it did for me.

Starting with verse 3, I want you to read the passage by putting in the specific name of another person where it says "us."

Here is how it would sound if you read it by putting in my name.

"Blessed be the God and Father of our Lord Jesus Christ, who has blessed Juan Carlos Ortiz with every spiritual blessing in the heavenly places in Christ, just as He chose Juan

Carlos Ortiz in Him before the foundation of the world, that Juan Carlos Ortiz should be holy and blameless before Him. In love He predestined Juan Carlos Ortiz to adoption as a son through Jesus Christ to Himself, according to the kind intention of His will, to the praise of the glory of His grace, which He freely bestowed upon Juan Carlos Ortiz in the Beloved. In Him Juan Carlos Ortiz has redemption through His blood, the forgiveness of his trespasses, according to the riches of His grace, which He lavished upon Juan Carlos Ortiz.''

If you are having difficulty accepting someone else, read the whole chapter putting that person's name in.

Did you realize that this person was such an important individual? By substituting the names of other people we don't like too well, we would fall in love with many tremendous personalities.

I am not telling you something that I think would be nice; I am telling you something that became a real-life experience to me. This has become a part of me. I did this, and now it is easy for me to accept people as they are, even if they appear to be unlikeable.

Once I met a person to whom I said, "Oh, Brother, I'm so pleased to meet you. Praise the Lord!"

He said, "Get out. I don't like you."

I said, "Yes, but I love you."

He said, "You cannot love me, because I am your enemy."

I said, "Alleluia! Lord, thank you that I have an enemy right in front of me to hug."

You will never go wrong loving.

That is why Jesus said we are to love even our enemies. We are not to love because a person is lovable; we are to love even the unlovable. We are to love as God loved us. Those who are introverted, those who are shy, those who have complexes, those whom we would like to avoid—these are the people God loves.

Why don't we love them?

Because we too often love with the same love that the

world loves with. And Jesus said that if we love only those who love us, we are no better than the world because it does that, too. We have to love as He loved us, simply because He is love and dwells within us to love through us.

Once you have seen the depth of God's love for you, you will be able to love and accept yourself. And when you have accepted yourself, you will be able to love others. It will not be a struggle, it will come easily. Because Jesus, who is love, lives in you, you will not be able to stop yourself from loving.

No wonder God gave us a command to love as He has loved us, because Jesus lives within us to be that love through us.

Praise God for His boundless love!